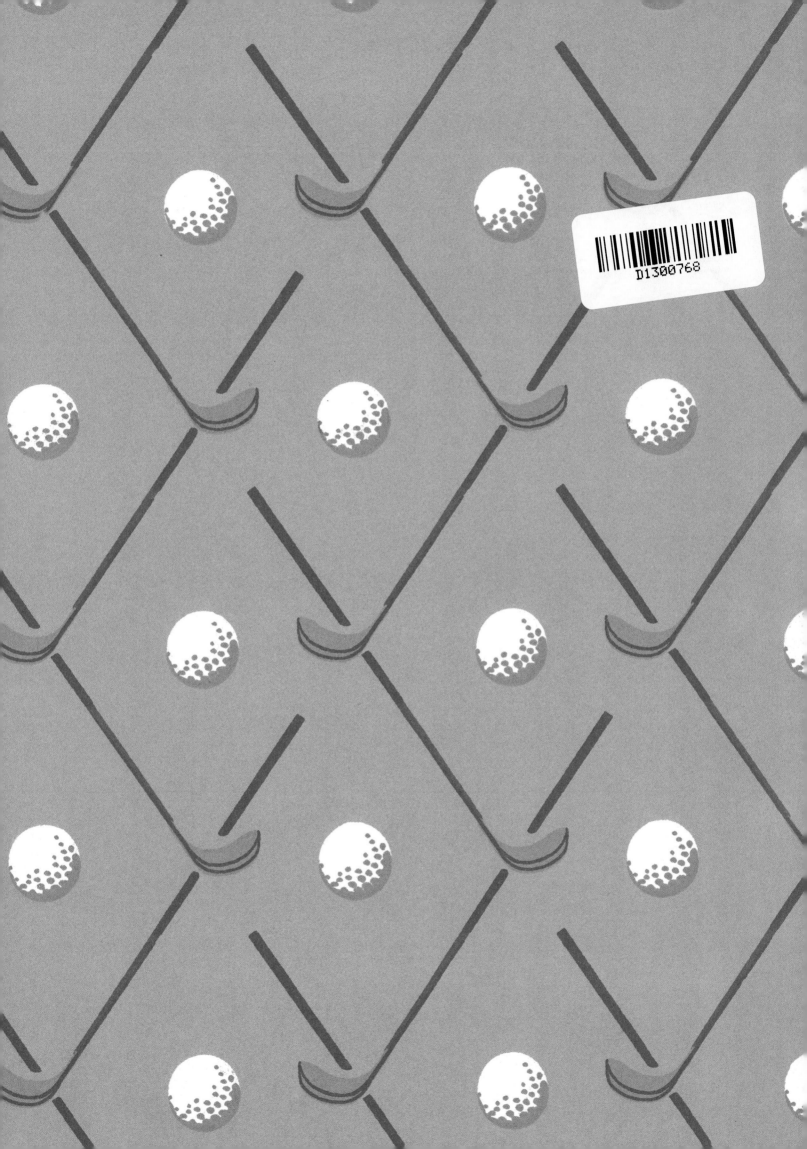

GOLF

STYLE

GOLF STYLE

Homes and Collections
Inspired by the Course and the Clubhouse

VICKY MOON

Photography by John Gessner, Ezra Gregg, and Vicky Moon
Design by Dina Dell'Arciprete/dk Design Partners Inc.

Clarkson Potter/Publishers
New York

ALSO BY VICKY MOON
The Official Middleburg Life Cookbook
Best Dressed Southern Salads
The Middleburg Mystique
A Sunday Horse
The Private Passion of Jackie Kennedy Onassis
Equestrian Style

Published in the United States by Clarkson Potter/Publishers, an imprint of the Crown
Publishing Group, a division of Random House, Inc., New York.
www.crownpublishing.com
www.clarksonpotter.com

CLARKSON POTTER is a trademark and POTTER with colophon is a registered trademark of Random House, Inc.

Library of Congress Cataloging-in-Publication Data
Moon, Vicky.
    Golf style / Vicky Moon. — 1st ed.
      p.   cm.
    Includes index.
    1. Collectibles in interior decoration.   2. Golf—Miscellanea.   I. Title.
NK2115.5.C58M665   2010
747—dc22   2010005652

ISBN 978-0-307-46023-3

Printed in China

Endpapers image courtesy of Thibaut, Inc.
This spread: *Royal Troon* by Sam Ingwersen
For a complete list of illustration credits, see page 252.

10 9 8 7 6 5 4 3 2 1

First Edition

CONTENTS

PART II THE BACK NINE

The love of golf arises from a sense of a peaceful place and a connection with stunning surroundings. It's the challenge of hitting a tiny white sphere to precise locations while retaining one's composure. It's the camaraderie between friends, spouses, business associates, and sometimes even total strangers finding common ground in a game they love.

And it's also about the competition—trying to beat the opponent, but ultimately testing one's own skills against the elements, the course, and inner demons.

Even with all the physical and emotional obstacles golf presents, its allure does not end as one enters the comfort of the clubhouse after a round of eighteen holes. The innumerable hues of green, from the trees to the highly manicured putting surfaces, appear frequently in clubhouse and golf resort decor; and inspired golfers now desire to enfold themselves at home with the same verdant tints and tones. The signature tartans from the founding fathers of golf in Scotland are evident on sofas, and golf motifs decorate wall coverings, window

OPPOSITE, CLOCKWISE FROM TOP LEFT: At Whistling Straits in Kohler, Wisconsin, golfers must walk the links-inspired course, as no carts are allowed. *William Inglis* by David Allan. Layering is the key to fashion and comfort for ladies facing changing temperatures and the elements while playing a friendly game of eighteen holes. Handsome wood-paneled locker rooms offer refuge after a tough day on the course.

treatments, and accessories, such as those found in the family home of 2007 British Amateur champion Drew Weaver.

For many people, the inspiration to surround themselves with all things golf begins with lessons at a local public course. The memory of its moist morning air lingers for a lifetime. Just ask any golfer where he or she learned to play: The answer might be more involved than anticipated, the recollections vivid.

Then there are the hours of lessons and endless practice sessions on the driving range, where a high-pitched ping and a baritone whack are followed intermittently by a staccato four-letter word. The whim of a somewhat innocent outing on an obscure course slowly grows into fascination, then progresses to fixation, obsession, and finally delight.

In the pages of this book, we will set out on our own round of eighteen chapters (plus refreshments at the nineteenth hole) to visit the homes of famous golfers, take a peek at priceless golf-themed art and antique collections, and explore how golf lovers eat, sleep, and breathe the sport.

We'll explore the homes of several professional golfers, such as champion Fred Funk, who solved the dilemma of how to spend more time with the family and still practice his short game by installing a putting green in his backyard. We'll visit passionate amateur participants, who read up on the latest techniques and buy state-of-the-art drivers that can be turbocharged with an infusion of hydrogen in the club head. Unwilling to leave their golf clubs in the bag, they seek to collect golf accoutrements not only for play, but also to decorate their homes. We find them here converted from an instrument (or some might say a weapon) into art, an imaginative sculpture, or furniture for the home.

Golf art also figures prominently in extending the pleasure at home, offering an imaginary substitute for being out on the course. A peek inside the walls of the New Jersey office of acclaimed course designer Rees Jones or the St. Simons Island home of champion Jonathan Byrd reveals they are filled with golf artwork. The paintings of such historical luminaries as Childe Hassam, Charles Edmund Brock, and Harry Rountree and contemporaries like Arthur Weaver, LeRoy Neiman, and Henry Koehler, all of whose work is pictured within this volume, evoke memories of the atmosphere of major championships, or perhaps document the vacation of a lifetime.

Out on the professional tour, at Doral, St. Andrews, or Pebble Beach, galleries hold their collective breath over the intensity of the putt as Sergio, Phil, Rocco, or Tiger, swathed in the latest fashions, stoops to study the line of the hole and the cut of a seemingly smooth green. Their admirers bedeck themselves with colorful pants, ties, and visors on and off the course. We'll chat with professional golfer Ian Poulter about his flamboyant style and we'll tell the story of Loudmouth men's pants worn by the outrageous and colorful John Daly.

Now that golf style extends to female fashion as well, observers of Lorena, Michelle, or Paula assert that the proper shirt and pants can even be worn shopping on the avenue or to an informal dinner on the patio. This volume also offers a peek at pastel scarves, needlepoint shoes, glittering golf jewels, and the wardrobe of Swedish-born golf star Sophie Gustafson.

And finally, what better way to celebrate the holidays than to bring a pine tree from outside into a cozy hearth? Golf insinuates itself seamlessly into a seasonal fete as floral designer Betty Ann Trible dresses her old Virginia home up to the "nines" with golf-themed ornaments and a golf-festooned mantel.

With a hint of pine scent lingering in the air, can springtime be far off? Never mind the sugarplums; for golfers it's visions of the pink azaleas in Augusta that must tide them over until they can begin playing again next season, or a dip into the pages of a book filled with all things golf.

OPPOSITE, ABOVE: President John F. Kennedy out for a game of golf at the Hyannis Country Club in Hyannis Port, Massachusetts, on August 17, 1963. OPPOSITE, BELOW: Among the numerous items that make colorful golf collectibles are the ball markers players use to hold a spot on the green while lining up a putt.

THE GOLFER'S SONG

To the tune of "The Armorer's Song" from *Robin Hood*.

Let iron on the white ball ring,

While the sunbeams brightly shine.

Let the world wag away

While I may play

This noble game of mine.

The club is the weapon to conquer fields;

I honor the man who makes it.

But the happy man is he who wields

It when into his grasp he takes it.

Let iron on the white ball ring, ring, ring,

While the sunbeams brightly shine,

Swing, ring, swing,

Then huzzah for the club and the links and the game,

Huzzah for the flying ball,

Let each tongue praise the name

And each cup pledge the fame

Of the game we love and extol.

—Francis Bowler Keene

THE F

PART I

RONT NINE

1

DORNOCH COTTAGE

Carol and Robert Hansen found the ultimate home for their extensive collection of golf antiques when they moved into Dornoch Cottage in Pinehurst, North Carolina. Situated inconspicuously along a pine tree–lined road, it backs up to the third hole of the acclaimed course known throughout the world simply as No. 2.

The 1925 two-story brick and frame structure is the former home of the esteemed golf course designer Donald Ross. The cottage is named after the wind-swept dunes along the Dornoch Firth in the distant northern reaches of his native Scotland. Responsible for nearly four hundred courses in the United States, including Pinehurst No. 2, Ross first came to the soft pine straw–laden Sandhills of North Carolina in 1900 as a golf professional and later became a course designer. His name is now synonymous with immense accomplishment. There's even a Donald Ross Society of admirers devoted to preserving his

oeuvre and experiencing his classic courses, known for simple elegance topped off with treacherous turtleback greens. Ross was also a founder and the first president of the American Society of Golf Course Architects in 1947.

Entering the foyer of Dornoch Cottage through its leaded-glass French front doors offers a preview of sparkling treasures to come. At every angle and level there is one flawless, artistic, and graceful display after another. A vintage black-and-white photograph of Donald Ross and his second wife, Florence Blackinton, sits in an alcove, giving a subdued indication of the history within these walls. Nearby, an unsigned 1920s watercolor *The Laird of the Links,* is purposefully placed at eye level.

The welcoming vignette includes a small version of *The Putter Boy,* an iconic sculpture by an unknown artist that sits behind the country club that is part of the Pinehurst Resort. On the left wall, the 1894 painting by Robert Nesbitt of *The Hell Bunker at the 14th Hole of the Old Course* completes the introduction.

Visitors' eyes are soon drawn into the light-filled formal living room. The pale yellow plaster walls were scarffed in a random pattern using a trowel to add a handsome texture. A mid-eighteenth-century hand-carved, two-tone walnut server with raised panels is tucked in along the far wall. "It fit perfectly between the doors that open to the back," Carol says. "This is a tough home to decorate, it's all windows and doors," adds Bob.

Inside the server is a collection of circa 1911–1933 Royal Doulton Golf Series Ware, with appropriate serving pieces: a platter, a bowl, a pitcher, and more. A rare Golf Series Ware punch bowl with fluted handles, a brass alloy tea caddy circa 1910–1920, and a contemporary (1970) bronze of Young Tom Morris (done by an unknown Edinburgh sculptor and later reproduced by Alexander Kirkwood & Son) sit on top of the server.

The remarkable painting above the server, *An Old Hoylake Group* by British major Francis Powell Hopkins (1830–1913), was completed in 1876. Hopkins is credited as the first artist to portray golfers in action. After serving in the army, he married and settled down in the seaside village along the north Devon coast known as Westward Ho!, named after the 1855 novel by Charles Kingsley. The 1864 Royal North Devon golf course is noted as the first English-style seaside links. Writing for *The Field* magazine under the name Shortspoon (a golf-club equal to today's three wood, for which he had a fondness), Hopkins signed his watercolors as Major Shortspoon or Major S.

PAGES 14 TO 15: British artist Nicholas Wanostrocht's *Golfing Scene.* PREVIOUS PAGE: Players on the third hole of Pinehurst No. 2 can be spotted from the rear gardens of Dornoch Cottage. ABOVE: Manufactured between 1911 and 1933, Royal Doulton Golf Series Ware is highly collectible. OPPOSITE: A light-filled corner shows off the pale yellow plaster walls scarfed in a random pattern using a trowel. The needlepoint chair is a family heirloom, and an English fruitwood rolltop desk dates to 1860. The circa-1915 to -1920 painting is by an American artist.

CLOCKWISE FROM TOP LEFT: The rear view of Dornoch Cottage today. The Hansens are not hesitant to use their antique Royal Doulton Golf Series Ware, such as the bowl holding a houseplant on the sideboard. A brass alloy tea caddy circa 1910–1920, a rare Royal Doulton Golf Series Ware punch bowl with fluted handles, and a contemporary bronze of Young Tom Morris are displayed atop a mid-eighteenth-century hand-carved, two-tone walnut server under Major Francis Powell Hopkins's painting *An Old Hoylake Group.* The original version of Dornoch Cottage.

CLOCKWISE FROM TOP LEFT: Donald Ross, the father of American golf architecture. On the dining table, red Gerber daisies fill an antique silver bowl adorned with a golf scene. The Hansens have attended to many details. They own a smaller version of *The Putter Boy* sculpture located behind the Pinehurst country club. The Royal Perth Match Book from 1874–1889 has been signed by notable members and guests including Old Tom Morris, Bob Andrews, and Major General Robert Boothby.

The more significant oil paintings, which are highly sought after today, were signed F. P. Hopkins.

A pair of pale pink upholstered armchairs adds an intentional dated ambiance to the living room environment. "There are so many straight lines in this room, we sought out pieces such as the chairs and smaller tables with curved soft lines," Carol explains. When the Hansens moved into Dornoch Cottage in 2002, they had the dark oak floors lightened to a pale honey. "Bob wanted heart pine, but I talked him out of it. I wanted to keep it original," she adds. An 1850 Persian Sultanabad rug with a bold rose-hued floral design balances the geometrics of the room.

Dating to 1860, an English fruitwood rolltop desk with a sliding leather top and satinwood drawers with ebony knobs is nestled into a light-filled corner. The Royal Perth Match Book from 1874–1889 rests on top. The treasured artifact lists members of the Scottish golf club and visiting golf professionals, including luminaries such as Old Tom Morris, Bob Andrews, and Major General Robert Boothby. "Boothby was noted for saving the game prior to 1850, when Scotland was in ruins after years of religious conflict," Bob notes. "He invested in restoring golf courses and communities as the industrial revolution gave new life and time to enjoy golf."

The vast great room across the back of the house gives way to the dining room, which overlooks a kitchen garden the Hansens have re-created using many of the same plants ordered by Donald Ross in 1934. During renovations, the couple chanced upon a handwritten order for 120 spring and summer perennials from Lancaster, Pennsylvania, all for $6.

At the opposite end of the house, a cozy library boasts a batch of heart pine floorboards that Donald Ross salvaged from a nearby 1888 house long before the notion of recycling became popular. Ross used the boards for walls when adding the library in 1936. Soft leather chairs invite one to sink in deep while admiring an oversize chalk-and-pencil study of a man called Fiery who served as three-time British Open champion Willie Park Jr.'s assistant.

Completed in 1894 by the artist James Marshall, such a portrait was unusual during the era, when most golf art highlighted the countryside. "Marshall had a personal affection for the sport, the people, and the personalities," Bob relates. "Fiery had a take-no-prisoners attitude; he could give some evil looks to the competition, and it comes through in this painting."

The intertwining stories depicted in Dornoch Cottage bring to life many precious items, such as a pencil sketch detail for the watercolor by Scottish artist J. Michael Brown (1854–1957) of the 1901 Women's Amateur Championship at Aberdovy in Wales, originally produced for the Life Association of Scotland calendar. Both pieces are framed attractively and hung unobtrusively on adjacent walls in the library.

Donald Ross's tiny former home office holds part of a collection of antique clubs, old golf course maps,

OPPOSITE: Players on Pinehurst No. 2 might find themselves face-to-face with this whimsical garden statue while searching for stray balls in the backyard of Dornoch.

magazines, and prints. Letters are displayed in a golf-themed silver-plated toast rack, a pedestal stereo-scope sits on a leather-top desk, and a vintage notion is accomplished with a replica telephone. There's no hint of a laptop, a flatbed scanner, or an iPod in the space Bob now uses.

What began innocently as a hobby four decades ago when he began accumulating golf balls and clubs has matured into a cunning collector's way of life. The Hansens' search for the elusive trophy, paint-ing, or book has since taken a different road. Auc-tion houses in London and Scotland that Bob once visited now make headlines when selling golf-related antiques, and the competition among collectors has become very keen. His reputation as a serious col-lector is acknowledged, and he doesn't participate as often as he once did.

Bob discloses that most extraordinary articles are now offered to him with a simple discreet phone call. "The rarest items are traded quietly and privately," he says, adding, "although by tradition, multigenera-tional old-money families have always deaccessed by auction. They'd never advertise."

Although the Hansens feel that their collection is now more or less complete, there are exceptions to their self-imposed rule not to seek out more items. An exquisite 1830s Chippendale-style mirror hangs in the foyer. While traveling recently, the Hansens could not resist an unscheduled peek in a roadside antique gallery in Charlotte, North Carolina, where they discovered the mirror.

"It's not what you're going to find; you can find anything," Bob advises, "It's about what you might miss and you can't always go back."

PREVIOUS PAGES: Major Francis Powell Hopkins's remarkable painting *An Old Hoylake Group,* completed in 1876, has been restored to its original glory. Hopkins signed his watercolors as Major Shortspoon or Major S, and his oil paintings, such as this one, were signed as F. P. Hopkins. **ABOVE:** *The Golf-Book of East Lothian,* published in 1896, notes that the silver bowl now on the dining room table was presented on December 19, 1885, as a wedding gift to Mr. H. W. Hope, owner of part of the land of the Luffness Golfing Ground in Scotland.

ABOVE: A tall wood box (a forerunner of modern golf shipping carriers) propped against the library wall bears the initials of golf historian H. S. C. Everard. The golf clubs inside bear the initials of Everard's father-in-law, Robert T. Boothby, the very same gentleman noted in the Royal Perth Match Book on the living room desk. **RIGHT:** Florence and Donald Ross spent a great deal of time in the library after it was added in 1936. Once floorboards, the heart pine walls were salvaged from a nearby 1885 house. On the back wall, the circa-1894 chalk and pencil drawing by James Marshall depicts one of the most famous caddies in history. Known as Fiery, "he could give some evil looks to the competition," Bob Hansen relates. "He had a take-no-prisoners look." **BELOW:** There's not even a hint of a laptop, a flatbed scanner, or an iPod in Donald Ross's former office space in Pinehurst.

On the Ice, in the Sheep Meadow, and to the Moon

2

The passion to pursue the great game of golf has gripped princes and presidents, schoolboys and scholars, weekend country clubbers, pitch-and-putt plebeians, and even an astronaut.

First called *suigan* or *chuiwan*, a stick-and-ball game similar to contemporary golf was played in China as early as during the Song Dynasty (960–1279). Artwork during the Ming Dynasty (1368–1644) shows women playing a derivation of the game indoors. Each player used ten clubs, some inlaid with gold and jade.

In the Netherlands, *kolf* was played on the ice and on dry land by hitting a leather ball with a stick— an ancient hybrid of a golf club and a hockey stick— around 1297. The idea migrated to Scotland via an active fourteenth- to seventeenth-century trade with the Netherlands, and the pronunciation evolved from *kolf* to *gowf* to *golf*.

A January 25, 1552, Scottish document granted local shepherds the right to graze sheep on the grounds at St. Andrews. The golf course was laid out along the shore of St. Andrews Bay and the estuary of the River Eden, with the natural flow of the land linking one hole to the next (hence the word *links*). There were eleven holes played out from the start and back for a total of twenty-two holes. In 1764, twenty-two were reduced to eighteen, which then became the worldwide standard. Visitors today will find countless challenging seaside courses in this charming corner of the world, and grazing sheep can still be spotted on a few of them.

One of the oldest Scottish golf clubs is the circa 1774 Musselburgh Links in East Lothian, where the Old Club Cup is still in competition.

The Oakhurst Links in the West Virginia village of White Sulphur Springs were constructed in 1884 as the first golf course in the United States. Complete with grazing sheep and still in use today, the course, within miles of the legendary circa 1778 Greenbrier resort, requires players to use the replica longnose clubs and gutty balls set up on sand tees.

THE OLDEST KNOWN GOLF SOCIETIES

1735 Royal Burgess Golfing Society
1744 Honourable Company of Edinburgh Golfers
1745 Royal Blackheath Golf Club
1754 Royal and Ancient Golf Club of St. Andrews
1761 Bruntsfield Links Golfing Society
1774 Royal Musselburgh Golf Club
1780 Royal Aberdeen Golf Club
1786 Crail Golfing Society
1787 Glasgow Golf Club
1797 Burntisland Golf House Club

PAGE 29: George Herbert Walker, great-grandfather of President George W. Bush, was president of the United States Golf Association in 1920. The biannual Walker Cup is named in his honor. **OPPOSITE, CLOCKWISE FROM TOP LEFT:** Grammy-award winner Justin Timberlake also likes to get 'N Sync at his Mirimichi Golf Course. Crooner Bing Crosby and comedian Bob Hope adored the game on the screen and on the road. Academy Award–winner Jack Nicholson plays in charity tournaments and practices on his own range above Beverly Hills. Astronaut Alan Shepard with the club he designed for his famous moon shot. Shinnecock Hills Golf Club, Southampton, New York, circa 1900. Michael Jordan loves not only basketball and baseball but also golf. The first photo of golf in America, at Saint Andrew's Golf Club, Yonkers, New York, 1888. **ABOVE RIGHT:** Newport Country Club, circa 1925. **BELOW RIGHT:** Grace Coolidge, left, and Florence Harding during the 1921 U.S. Open championship at Columbia Country Club, Chevy Chase, Maryland.

PREVIOUS PAGES: The 1900 Yale golf team. TOP: Harry Vardon at St. Andrews, Scotland, as Old Tom Morris (at left in long coat) looks on, 1890s. ABOVE: Sheep grazing in front of The Country Club, Brookline, Massachusetts, circa 1900. OPPOSITE: Robert Goetzl's illustration *Moon Shot* celebrates the twenty-fifth anniversary of Alan Shepard's outer-space drive.

Scottish immigrant John Reid, often referred to as "the Father of American Golf," launched a course in a cow pasture near Yonkers, New York, in 1888 and became president of The Saint Andrew's Golf Club. The earliest members assembled on a bench surrounding an apple tree and became known as "the Apple Tree Gang."

The Country Club in Brookline, Massachusetts, established in 1882, was the first private golf club in the United States. The United States Golf Association, first known as the Amateur Golf Association, was formed twelve years later in 1894. Charter member clubs included the Newport Golf Club, the Shinnecock Hills Golf Club, The Country Club of Brookline, Saint Andrew's Golf Club in Yonkers, and the Chicago Golf Club. To put the sport in historical context, the first Ford Model T appeared fourteen years later.

Technology and the game had both greatly advanced by the time golf enthusiast Alan Bartlett Shepard Jr. lifted off to the moon on January 31, 1971, with a golf club stowed away in his gear on *Apollo 14*.

The astronaut later credited comedian and golf devotee Bob Hope for the idea. While hosting a television show at NASA headquarters in 1970, as members of the crew were becoming acquainted with the change in gravity, Hope went up on a high-wire training device similar to the one used by Mary Martin in the original Broadway production of *Peter Pan*. As he lifted off the ground, the comedian placed his ever-present driver down to act as a tripod and that image planted the first seed for the moon shot.

"With uncharacteristic immodesty, I must take credit for the inspiration that produced Alan Shepard's famous golf shot on the moon," Hope wrote with typical tongue-in-cheek humor in his book *Confessions of a Hooker: My Lifelong Love Affair with Golf*.

Shepard even helped design a special club for his historic lunar shot. NASA engineers fashioned four pieces of aluminum normally used for geological exploration into a six iron, which folded up like a telescope. The late astronaut's first swing on the Fra Mauro region hit a clump of moondust. The NASA transmission to earth was: "Got more dirt than ball. Here we go again."

No official yardage was ever reported, but like many golfers, Shepard had an excellent excuse for the lack of distance: "Because of the cumbersome suit I was wearing, I couldn't make a very good pivot on the swing and I had to hit the ball with just one hand." Shepard later retired to the California golf mecca of Pebble Beach, and the club is now part of the collection housed at the United States Golf Association in Far Hills, New Jersey.

HOME ON THE RANGE

When professional golfer Denis Watson bought a home in the mid-1990s along a canal in a South Florida neighborhood, he strategically incorporated a place to practice on the property. Plans also called for a glass office for his wife, attorney Susan Loggans, overlooking the patio and waterway, ample play space for their five young children, and a workroom where Denis could repair and store his equipment.

A native of Rhodesia (now known as Zimbabwe), Denis has demonstrated what sheer determination and dedication can do for a golfer. On the American PGA Tour in 1984, Denis posted three victories, tying for the most wins on the tour that season. The next year, when Denis hit a tree root while swinging a club, he suffered a severe neck, elbow, and wrist injury, resulting in numerous surgeries. He was told he'd never play again, and after several attempts at a return, he retired. Twenty-three years later, he made what has been acknowledged as one of the greatest comebacks of all time when he captured the 2007 Senior PGA Championship at Kiawah Island. He's since become a regular on the Champions Tour for players over fifty.

To continue fine-tuning his skills, Denis installed a maintenance-free artificial turf putting green within steps of his back door. Just across the pool next to the seawall, a net-enclosed area serves as a place for Denis to practice.

At the end of the day, Denis often retreats to his workroom to repair and refurbish his clubs. Once a garage bay, the space was easily adapted to meet his needs with recessed shelves to hold clubs, a work table for tools, and ample wall space for photos recording his gritty career.

3

BRUSHSTROKES

From wide, sweeping vistas to stately portraits, from intricate pieces of equipment and colorful clothing to blissful bursts of victory, golf offers continual inspiration to artists past and present. They have captured the hushed and graceful

nature of the game on paper, board, and canvas in oil, pastels, and watercolor.

Discovering that perfect piece of art presents a challenge almost equal to making par on the seventh hole at Pebble Beach. "The sheer scarcity is a factor," says art dealer Greg Ladd of Lexington, Kentucky. "In thirty-five years, only one significant historical piece has crossed my path, and that was by British artist Major Francis Powell Hopkins. "And in today's market there are just very few artists who specialize in golf." According to one collector, "Golf started as a pedestrian game. There simply wasn't a great demand for expensive art. As the sport was adopted by the wealthy, the golf art market gained momentum." As with the game, many intrepid collectors delight in the challenge.

SWEEPING VISTAS AND STATELY PORTRAITS

Several early examples of golf art appear in Dutch paintings of the 1600s. The ice fields provide the backdrop where players strike the ball in a primitive version of the sport, then known as *kolf* or *colf*. Hendrick Avercamp (1585–1634) illuminated the frigid pastimes of winter life in an oil painting titled *Colf Players on the Ice*. Artist Adriaen van de Velde (1636–1672) followed when he captured the players against the skyline with a windmill in the distance in *Kolf on the Ice Near Haarlem*.

As the sport invaded the British Isles, the landscape also provided a setting for fashionable portraits in elegant golf attire. In the mid-1700s, Scottish artist William Mosman of Aberdeen portrayed Sir James Macdonald and Sir Alexander Macdonald in striking red sporting suits with golf clubs in hand.

Sir Henry Raeburn (1756–1823) is best known for his frequently reproduced work of an ice-skating rector, *Reverend Robert Walker Skating on Duddingston Loch*. His portraits of noted golf officials such as the secretary-treasurer of the Honourable Company of Edinburgh Golfers, James Balfour, Esq., as well as John Gray, the secretary of the Royal Company of Golfers, were later reproduced as engraved mezzotints in the early 1800s.

Painter Charles Lees (1800–1880), whom Raeburn mentored, was surrounded by golf courses in his hometown of Cupar in the county of Fife. Lees specialized in portraits and sporting subjects. One well-known oversize oil portrays a match between Sir David Baird and Sir Ralph Anstruther against Major Hugh Lyon Playfair and John Campbell of Saddell at the Old Course at the Royal and Ancient Golf Club in St. Andrews. It is often referred to as *The Golfers*, but the proper title is *A Grand Match Played Over*

PAGE 39: This portrait of Sir James Macdonald and Sir Alexander Macdonald dated 1749 is attributed to artist William Mosman. **OPPOSITE, TOP:** Known as *kolf* and played on ice fields, the game of golf as recorded by Dutch artist Adriaen van de Velde. **OPPOSITE, MIDDLE:** Often referred to as *The Golfers,* the proper title of this Charles Lees painting now in the National Galleries of Scotland is *The Grand Match Played Over St. Andrews Links.* **OPPOSITE, BOTTOM:** Painted by an unknown artist sometime between 1790 and 1800, this portrait of a British golfer is thought to have been inspired by the portrait of John Musters of Nottingham that the esteemed artist Sir Joshua Reynolds created between 1777 and 1780. **LEFT:** The red jackets of the golfers seen in this portrait by Lees indicate membership in a British club. **BELOW:** Harry Rountree's artwork appears in Bernard Darwin's highly collectible *Golf Courses of the British Isles.*

St. Andrews Links. It was commissioned by George Cheape, whose family owned all of the land of St. Andrews from 1667 and lived in a grand estate known as Strathtyrum, which is still in existence. The original painting was ultimately donated to the permanent collection at the National Galleries of Scotland, where Raeburn's famous skating painting also hangs. A copy remains at Strathtyrum.

Following the death of Sir Henry Raeburn in 1823, Sir John Watson Gordon (1788–1864) became the best-known portrait painter in Scotland. His regal portrait of John Taylor, clad in a red captain's jacket while his caddy tees up the ball, is one of the best known paintings in golf. The portrait was supposedly started by Raeburn and completed by Gordon.

Irishman Sir John Lavery (1856–1941) began as a photographer and became well known as a society portrait painter. His subjects included Queen Victoria, in an 1888 commission for the Glasgow International Exhibition. From 1921 to 1922, Lavery painted pictures of the golf course at North Berwick in East Lothian and was captivated by working en plein air. This links course, which extends from the town to the edge of the Firth of Forth, has fascinated artists since it was founded in 1832.

The oldest of four artist brothers, Charles Edmund Brock (1870–1938) began illustrating books at the age of twenty and went on to create images for works by Jane Austen, Jonathan Swift, and William Thackeray under the signature of C. E. Brock. His technique transitions readily from delicate prim and proper Victorian novels such as *Emma* to robust sporting figures on the golf course. An engraving of his 1894 painting of four golfers is part of the vast collection of art at the United States Golf Association headquarters in Far Hills, New Jersey.

One of the most revered golf artists, Harry Rountree (1878–1950) moved to England from New Zealand and began his career illustrating children's books at the age of twenty-three. In 1910, Rountree painted sixty-four golf landscape watercolors in collaboration with author Bernard Richard Meirion Darwin for the book *The Golf Courses of the British Isles.*

Harry Rountree's depiction of skies was influenced by the British landscape painter John Constable, "particularly his dramatic skies, which were seldom blue," according to retired architect turned golf artist Sam Ingwersen of Bexley, Ohio, who also has written about golf art. "Of the sixty-four originally published paintings by Rountree, only three have predominantly blue skies, and only seven fairways are colored predominantly green or yellow green."

Rountree's use of watercolor provided an illusion of transparency as light filters through trees and bounces off water hazards. "His depictions of the natural surrounds of bunkers, sand, and grass were enhanced by his mix of contrasting colors. His seas, puddles, and ponds were gleaming with reflections and light sparkling upon their surfaces," Sam Ingwersen describes.

OPPOSITE: This portrait of four-time Open Champion Thomas Mitchell Morris Sr. (1821–1908), known as Old Tom Morris, shows him along the pathway in his hometown of St. Andrews, Scotland, not far from his club-making shop and the 18th green. **ABOVE:** Painted by Scottish artist Allan Stewart in 1919, *The First International Foursome—England v. Scotland* is based upon an historic match between the Duke of York (later James II) and several English noblemen on the Leith Links in 1682. **LEFT:** Charles Edmund Brock's painting *The Putt* sold at Christie's South Kensington London auction of golf memorabilia in July 2000 for $57,039. Brock began work as an illustrator for writers such as Jane Austen, Jonathan Swift, and William Thackeray. This 1894 painting is signed as C. E. Brock.

SOFT LIGHT AND INTRICATE EQUIPMENT

The celebrated American Impressionist Childe Hassam (1859–1935) also was known for how his paintings captured subtle variations of light. Perhaps best known for his series of paintings of American flags along Fifth Avenue in New York City, the artist displayed his passion for golf in his work as well.

Beginning as a wood engraver and illustrator, Childe Hassam later traveled to Europe and worked in watercolor. By the 1890s, he had secured acclaim as one of America's foremost Impressionists.

The Hassams purchased a home in East Hampton near the stately Maidstone Club, where they were members. The artist swam daily and played golf frequently.

"The golf paintings are one of the best kept secrets about Hassam's work," says John Surovek, owner of the Surovek Gallery in Palm Beach. "Everyone knows the flag paintings, but only the true collectors of American Impressionist art know about the golf."

In 2008, Surovek Gallery had in its inventory a 1907 golf painting called *Wainscott Links*, which had been in the same family for more than fifty years. "It's rare for such a painting to become available," John adds. "Some of his paintings have sold for ten to twelve million dollars."

The noted Impressionist completed more than a dozen golf paintings in the charming Long Island village. The atmosphere near the sea and the vernacular architecture of shingled cottages held a place in Childe Hassam's heart until his death in 1935.

Long before the Hamptons became a chic weekend hot spot, it was an artists' colony. Just as Childe Hassam was captivated, so too did octogenarian

OPPOSITE: American Impressionist Frederick Childe Hassam went beyond his well-known American flag settings on Fifth Avenue in New York City to paint *Morning on the Maidstone Links* on Long Island. **LEFT:** Henry Koehler's home and studio are tucked into a quiet spot amid the hubbub of Long Island. **BELOW LEFT:** The Duke of Devonshire once noted, "Because most of Henry's paintings are unfashionably small, they are often hung in slightly out-of-the-way places, but they always catch, and then hold, your eye." **BELOW RIGHT:** Sporting equipment of all types has always been a favorite subject for Henry Koehler.

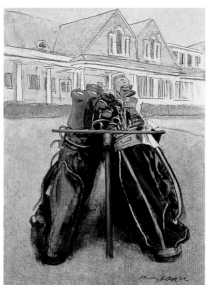

Henry Koehler find this an enchanting place to paint.

As a young boy growing up in Louisville, Henry started drawing on cardboard he found when his father's shirts came back from the laundry. While at Yale, he majored in art. His illustrations appeared in *Vogue, Fortune*, and *Harper's* magazines. He also did work for *Sports Illustrated*—a lot of golf and racing.

"I could see the writing on the wall that hand-drawn illustrations in magazines were on the way out and photography was going to eclipse everything else," he recalls. Gradually Henry switched to oil painting, favoring all things horse. The vibrant reds of a hunting jacket and the luminous palette of racing silks, including those of HRM Queen Elizabeth II, are dazzling. His patrons include Ambassador William Farish and HRH the Prince of Wales, as well as the late Jackie Kennedy Onassis, Paul Mellon, and Duchess of Windsor.

"I love equipment," the artist enthuses. "Just as with the paintings of boots and saddles, I approach golf from another direction." Instead of painting a large swath of a fairway or a green, he zooms in on the bags and clubs. Of his work, he says: "It tells a story in miniature."

London-born Arthur Weaver (1918–2008) produced larger canvases than Koehler but was similarly captivated by the elusive changes in light. His oil paintings of broad fairways and pristine greens brought to life such notable locations as the 360-yard seventeenth hole of the National Golf Links course, designed by the legendary Charles Blair Macdonald in Southampton, Long Island. Regarded as one of the leading talents in golf art, Weaver lived in Wales and traveled the world in pursuit of courses to depict.

COLORFUL CLOTHING AND BLISSFUL BURSTS

Instead of focusing on the landscape, Charo Aymerich concentrates on the players. A lifelong player with a current handicap of eight, she brings a familiarity with the game to her work: "My whole family plays; even my ninety-year-old mother plays twice a week at our club in Madrid, which my brother manages."

Now in Rotterdam, Charo has incorporated her enthusiasm into her oeuvre. She used a neighbor, a student at the University of Amsterdam, as a model for *Madera o Hierro?* and *Ultimo Hoyo.* "The angle of view was chosen to achieve a more anonymous view of the model. It could refer to many golf players," she explains. "In addition, the view is from below—this to avoid painting the course. I hate using green colors in portrait paintings. I prefer to have a sober background. What I call the color of emptiness."

For *Madera o Hierro?* Charo was attempting to capture the typical mood of any golf player: doubt. "Which club do I use? Long iron? Five wood?" In *Ultimo Hoyo,* the young man is heading to the final hole. "Like many of us, this player is not very satisfied with his score," she explains. "There's always that terrible triple bogey somewhere during the back nine."

For nonprofessional golfers, even a triple bogey rarely ruins a sunny day out on the links. Some call it a perfect day no matter the outcome. Lombard, Illinois, artist Karen Gehse's start in art came when she painted the still life *The Perfect Day* for her brother, Paul Underwood, a former golf pro.

Karen uses loose brushstrokes and works only in oils. "I love the landscapes; there are lots of colors that we don't imagine we're seeing outdoors, such as blue and orange and yellow grass, or purple and orange in the leaves of trees," she says.

No sports artist is more recognized for his robust use of color than octogenarian LeRoy Neiman. His vibrant works in watercolor, oil, and pastel are completed as silk-screen serigraphs, lithographs, etchings, and paintings and he also does pencil sketches on anything from a scorecard to a pairings sheet.

Neiman has followed golfers around the world, to the shrine of St. Andrews, as well as to Lake Tahoe, Hong Kong, Japan, France, and Palm Springs, and Pebble Beach, every golfer's ultimate dream venue.

When working on a golf painting, Neiman sees the clubhouse as the centerpiece. "It's unique and individual," he says. His canvases go on to explore the man-made and natural tests of water, topography, and sand, each one exploding in color.

Yet amid this kaleidoscopic riot, LeRoy Neiman concludes: "I aim to express the gentlemanly attitude of the game and the tranquil beauty of the landscape."

PREVIOUS PAGES: The gentle waves near the 13th hole at Pebble Beach were captured by Adriano Manocchia. **OPPOSITE, TOP:** Artist Guy Salvato deviated from his usual subtle images of the fairways in this large study in acrylic called *Tee It Up* for the dining area of his Pinehurst cottage. **OPPOSITE, BOTTOM:** Connoisseurs of fine golf art cherish the work of Arthur Weaver, such as his *Playing the 7th Green.* **ABOVE:** For her brother Paul Underwood, a former golf pro, Illinois artist Karen Gehse completed a still life, *The Perfect Day,* with golf accoutrements and a bottle of beer in a peaceful spot of grass.

NOTABLE GOLF ARTISTS

Sir Francis Grant (1803–1878)
Thomas Hodge (1827–1907)
John Smart (1838–1899)
Sir George Reid (1841–1913)
The Hon. John Collier (1850–1934)
John Charlesv Dolman (1851–1934)
Douglas Adams (1853–1920)
W. Dendy Sadler (1854–1923)
Cecil Aldin (1870–1935)
J. A. A. Berrie (1887–1962)
Everett Henry (1893–1961)

CLOCKWISE FROM TOP LEFT: LeRoy Neiman's kaleidoscopic colors come together for the 2008 Ryder Cup at the Valhalla Country Club in Kentucky. A young golfer contemplates whether he should use *Madera o Hierro?*—wood or iron—in Spanish artist Charo Aymerich's painting. Some may view the iconic clubhouse at St. Andrews as staid, but LeRoy Neiman brings it to life. A former graphics specialist, Guy Salvato now captures his favorite courses in oil. **OPPOSITE, CLOCKWISE FROM TOP LEFT:** The final hole—*Ultimo Hoyo*—by Aymerich. Karen Gehse finds inspiration at Butterfield Country Club in Illinois. This Art Deco-style print shows an endearing moment between generations. *Harbor Town* by Adriano Manocchia and *Safe Harbor* by Salvato.

4

Hot Pants and Spiffy Spikes

Golf style sometimes manifests itself from head to toe in men's sportswear worn on the golf course. Clothing worn during play has historically been conservative, from the traditional drab apparel worn in the British Isles to the humdrum khakis favored in the United States.

Today, the fashion statements made by professionals, and emulated by their fans, extend to slacks and shirts, hats and caps, and even shoes. Marketing psychology suggests that donning the same clothes as a successful professional might improve one's results. *Might.*

Two flashy seventy-something American professional golfers had fabulous results in leading a fashion revolution against the dull and dingy with their interpretation of style. A Southern playboy with a superb short swing, Doug Sanders has been dubbed "the Peacock of the Fairways" for his choice of vivid

"It has always interested me that these athletes wear the same attire as their galleries. They are not separated by uniforms or sports gear indicating team names or numbers." —Golf artist LeRoy Neiman

shades of chartreuse. Sanders once even dyed his socks and underwear to match.

South African native and fashion plate Gary Player, a three-time winner of both the Masters and the British Open, continues to wear all black on the links. His dark attire earned him the nickname "the Black Knight," and now other players can achieve this look with his clothing line, the Gary Player Collection.

Johnny Miller, a leading contender on the tour during the 1970s who had U.S. Open and British Open victories to his credit, came out swinging with an eclectic wardrobe built around a wide variety of plaid pants. After retiring in 1990, he began a new career as an outspoken golf analyst for NBC Sports and is now generally regarded as the best in the business.

The late Payne Stewart will forever be remembered for his bold and fearless wardrobe of plus fours. Bunched at four inches below the knee (hence the name), they are seen in traditional tartans, solid hues of khaki, and even bright red and royal blue. They should not be confused with the baggy knee-length knickers, short for knickerbockers. Stewart also had a long-term contract with the National Football League to wear the team colors of the closest franchise to the golf course he was playing.

LEAD WITH THE LEG

On today's international professional tour, Englishman Ian Poulter is making headlines with his golfing garb originally made by William Hunt, a Savile Row tailor in London. A world-class player on the PGA and European tours, Poulter won the 2000 Italian Open, the 2001 Moroccan Open, and the 2003 Celtic Manor Resort Wales Open, among other victories. At the British Open at Royal Troon in Ayrshire, Scotland, in July 2004, he appeared in pants resembling his country's Union Jack.

The fabric for Ian's pants was custom printed at Elanbach, a boutique factory at the estate of Llangoed Hall in Wales, which is owned by the family of the immensely popular late designer Laura Ashley and her late husband, Sir Bernard Ashley.

The well-known interior designer Annabel Elliot also used Elanbach fabrics when decorating the Carmarthenshire residence of Charles, HRH the Prince of Wales, and Camilla, HRH the Duchess of Cornwall.

Ian's pants incorporated the bespoke Elanbach materials for several years before he took it one step further and moved to manufacturing fabrics of his own vision. "I didn't realize the buzz that this would

PREVIOUS PAGE: It is now possible to coordinate one's wardrobe with matching grips and gloves. ABOVE: The late Payne Stewart can be credited with making plus fours an accepted form of golf attire. OPPOSITE: Ian Poulter made headlines around the world when he showed up in these pants.

CLOCKWISE FROM TOP LEFT: Each year the Royal and Ancient Golf Club issues a tie commemorating the site of the Open. This red jacket was worn by United States Ryder Cup team captain Sam Snead in 1969. Fore! Watch out for nattily dressed men in handsome ties, shirts, and sweaters.

LEFT: Stepping out onto the golf course in style with these capped-toe black-and-white spectators with rubber soles. After play they can easily be worn indoors. ABOVE: Replacing the original buttons on a tweed blazer with golf-motif buttons transforms the entire appearance. BELOW: A belt offers a reminder of a memorable "round" after visiting a very special course—and takes up very little room in a suitcase packed for the return home.

create. It was insane," he recalls of the 2007 launch of IJP (Ian James Poulter) Design.

The IJP line designed in Great Britain and produced in Great Britain, Morocco, and the Far East differs from the power red Nike shirt traditionally worn on Sundays by Tiger Woods and the wardrobe of Sergio Garcia from Adidas. Many of the top players wear a line of sports clothing from a manufacturer as part of a sponsorship. Each little collar, cap, and sleeve is available for corporate logo placement, which can be worth $10 million or more each year, and Ian has also struck several such placement deals.

For his line, Ian Poulter states, "I wanted to do something different and branch out." As a young man, he worked selling clothes and used his earnings to buy the latest fashions. While traveling the world playing golf, he frequently made sketches on any scrap of paper he could find.

For his team of a dozen employees in offices near his home in Northampton, Poulter handpicked Lucia Cowan and Sophie Snowball. The two women design and compile the color palettes, which "determine the mood and set the tone for the whole collection," according to Sophie. One of the choices is a striking all-white ensemble.

Subtle design elements include a boot-cut leg with a two-inch vent on the side seam so the pants sit neatly on top of the golf shoe, and a tiny ball marker pocket set within the larger front frog pocket. In keeping with the IJP philosophy of

Indigo

Indigo – 66

Bugatti Blue – 67

Sea Green – 68

Ocean Spray – 69

"leading with the leg," the overall design process begins with the color palette for three tartans of four colors each for the trousers. Each tartan is registered with the Scottish Tartan Authority and milled in Great Britain. Says Ian: "There's no other textile design in the world that allows the wearer to celebrate and proudly proclaim: 'I come from this country. This is my family . . . my clan . . . my city . . . district, company, regiment, college, football team, golf club. The list is almost endless.'"

OPPOSITE: While some golfers prefer to wear a traditional cap, others wear a visor. Professional Ian Poulter chooses from his own line of clothing but knows when to keep his head down and his eye on the ball. **ABOVE:** Tartan takes on an updated look with indigo blue.

OPPOSITE: Ian Poulter strides out on the course in jet-black and pure white tartan. **ABOVE AND RIGHT:** A touch of tartan in the form of a tie, fabric on a pillow, or a strategically placed wall covering offers golf style on the course and in the clubhouse.

TARTAN

Tartan, an ancient art form of a woven plaid pattern, dates to 700 BC and is now frequently associated with golf and seen on fabrics in clubhouses and fashionable sportswear around the world. Though the earliest evidence of tartan was found in southern Russia and China, it grew famous throughout Scotland as a result of various factors, including the westward expansion of the Celts as well as the later expansion of the Roman Empire. The Romans destroyed much of the Celtic tradition throughout Europe, but they were unable to conquer tribes located within the isolated Scottish Highlands. It was there that the tradition of tartan weaving would continue to grow for the following sixteen hundred years. What began as a tribal trend with less than 100 designs has flourished into a worldwide phenomena that now includes more than 4,000 patterns. Each year nearly 120 new designs are registered with the Scottish Tartan Authority.

LEFT: Even the little blue mark used to identify one's ball can match one's pants. **BELOW:** Brightly colored pants of all types bring smiles on the golf course even when the scorecard might not. **BOTTOM:** A young golfer in Loudmouth's "Disco Balls" pants, inspired by the loud pants worn in the movie *Caddyshack,* contemplates the afternoon at the very same tree featured in the film. Fictionally named Bushwood for the film, the course was originally called Rolling Hills and is now known as Grande Oaks.

WATCH OUT FOR GOPHERS

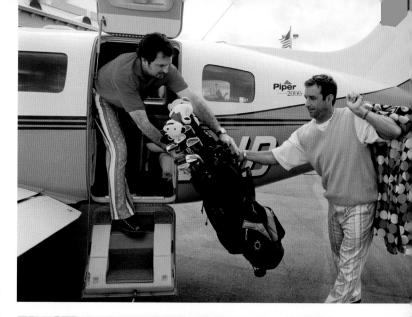

Like Ian Poulter, Scott "Woody" Woodworth was inspired to create unique golf fashion. "I remembered Johnny Miller's red and white pants. I wanted something like that," he declares.

"All I could find was khaki, blue, black, or gray and I thought, 'Why bother?'" Woody found his way to the children's aisle at Jo-Ann Fabrics. He bought three yards of powder blue material with Bugs Bunny, Daffy Duck, and the Tasmanian Devil in a golf cart swinging clubs. He had a pair of pants made.

"When I went out to play, someone said, 'Where'd you get those pants?' Everyone wanted a pair," says Woody, who studied at Brown and the Rhode Island School of Design. Then he started a website to sell his creations, calling it Loudmouth Golf.

He now travels the country selling and marketing the flamboyant pants in eye-popping digitally printed fabrics. The kaleidoscopic designs include "Disco Balls" and "Ticket-A-Tasket." There are also pants called "Rodney," a send-up of Rodney Dangerfield, who played the wild-pants-wearing part of loudmouth Al Czervik in the cult classic comedy *Caddyshack*. The name of the dazzling blue plaid pants, "Bushwood," will ring a bell with movie trivia buffs as the fictional moniker of Rolling Hills Golf Club in Davie, Florida, where the movie was filmed. (It is now known as Grande Oaks Country Club.) The large oak tree by the clubhouse might look very familiar. Warning to all golfers: watch out for gophers.

TOP AND BOTTOM: The fuselage of Loudmouth's corporate airplane matches the eye-popping colors of the clothing. Large geometric forms are printed directly onto the fabric. **MIDDLE:** As this colorful threesome played a friendly round of 18 holes at the Coral Ridge Country Club in Fort Lauderdale, they were greeted by fellow duffers with smiles and an endless barrage of inquiries as to where one might also acquire a pair of these effervescent pants.

FASHIONABLE LIDS

Fashion does not begin and end with the shirt and pants. Golfers also make a statement with their hats, as Payne Stewart did with his coordinating tam-o'-shanter. Swede Jesper Parnevik used to wear his caps with the front bill flipped up, and later switched to a modified black straw porkpie number often referred to as a "Chicago mob hat." Ricky Barnes, who tied for second at the 2009 U.S. Open, began wearing a painter's cap, mostly because his head didn't perspire quite as much as in a traditional golf cap. The legendary Sam Snead's original fedora was made of coconut straw, and the late Jimmy Demaret donned a Swiss yodeler's hat during the mid-1940s.

THE AGONY OF THE FEET

Just as wearing the same shirt as Sergio Garcia will not improve a duffer's score, donning a pair of golf shoes like those worn by any big-name professional golfer will not make even a one-stroke difference. On the other hand, the right shoe can improve a player's game. Ben Hogan's seemingly smooth swing was considered to be the secret to his forty-six victories on the PGA Tour during the 1940s and '50s. However, the key to his success may well have been hidden: Hogan had an extra spike inserted on the ball of his right shoe to ensure additional traction and thus better control.

The fact that most people have one foot larger than the other is also worth pondering. An incorrectly fitted golf shoe, pinching a heel or rubbing an instep, can cause one to lose concentration on a critical swing or putt. The late, great Sam Snead, who more than occasionally played barefoot, once said that golf got complicated when he had to wear shoes.

Some golfers prefer custom-made golf shoes in order to accommodate the difference in foot size or narrow heels and to cushion the ankle. E. Vogel, a family-owned business based in New York City since 1879, has the answer.

"We take six measurements," explains Hank Vogel, an avid golfer himself. These include the ball, instep, waist of the foot, heel, and length, and an outline of the foot. "We want to know how high or low your arch is," he explains. He recommends a rubber ribbed sole, an even newer variation on the soft

ABOVE LEFT: A fedora fashioned of coconut straw was Sam Snead's signature hat. ABOVE RIGHT: For the 1913 U.S. Open championship, young caddy Eddie Lowery wore a simple golf bucket hat and Francis Ouimet donned a traditional tweed cap. OPPOSITE: Now a television golf personality, Johnny Miller was noted for his colorful wardrobe and even his fashion-forward statement of plaid pants when competing on the tour and winning the U.S. Open and British Open in the 1970s.

spikes. "It gives very nice balance when you set up for your swing."

The average delivery time for the first pair is three months. The second pair takes about two months, with the cost ranging from $650 to $6,000.

For those who might want to spend less, FootJoy offers customized selections through the MyJoys program. It allows golfers to custom build their shoes with hundreds of color, design, logo, and personalization options. The final tab is anywhere from $250 to $3,000, which was well worth it to Argentinean Angel Cabrera, winner of the 2009 Masters after a dramatic sudden-death play-off against Kenny Perry and Chad Campbell (also in FootJoys).

World-class players like Fred Couples, Stuart Appleby, and Colin Montgomerie have worn shoes from the Danish shoe company Ecco. As the only major golf shoe maker to own its tanneries and production facilities, they boast "from cow to consumer." Ecco also claims that their golf shoes "feature a network of built-in technologies to create the ideal platform for the perfect swing."

Australian Greg Norman has a long and flowing swing no matter what type of shoes he wears. The Hall of Famer held the number one spot in the world for

three hundred weeks in the 1980s and early 1990s, but he could never blame his three well-documented Masters defeats on a shoe malfunction or a pinched toe.

In 1986, Norman had the lead going into the final eighteen holes, and Jack Nicklaus beat him by a shot. A year later, he lost in a sudden-death play-off against Larry Mize. In 1996, he held a six-shot lead going into the final round, then suffered the worst loss in Masters history, losing to Englishman Nick Faldo.

"It was a huge turning point in my life," the Aussie has said. "I was elevated in the world of the public eye by losing, not by winning. That changed my life, I can tell you that, just from the outpouring of e-mails and letters and support that I got. So I won in a lot of ways, but I didn't win the green jacket."

He now focuses on designing golf courses, on producing world-class wine, and on overseeing his vast line of apparel, the Greg Norman Collection,

Alas, no matter how nattily one is kitted out on the field or off, apparel is no assurance of golf glory.

LOGO LAND

Shark—Greg Norman
Golden Bear—Jack Nicklaus
Umbrella—Arnold Palmer
Lion—John Daly
Walrus—Craig Stadler
Pink Panther—Paula Creamer

OPPOSITE: Most people have two different-sized feet; some solve the problem by ordering custom-made golf shoes. ABOVE: Shoe expert and avid golfer Hank Vogel recommends ribbed rubber soles in order to set up balance and improve your swing.

SOME PEOPLE JUST DON'T BELONG

Golf has been the focal point of a wide variety of Hollywood films over the years, as far back as the Three Stooges competing for laughs on the links in the 1930s. Bob Hope almost always took his sticks "on the road" with Bing Crosby (to Morocco, Zanzibar, and Singapore), and managed a round of golf with Arnold Palmer when he played himself in *Call Me Bwana.* For *The Caddy* in 1953, Dean Martin and Jerry Lewis took the sport to new heights of hilarity.

Sean Connery's fascination with golf was sparked in 1964 while he was playing the part of 007 in the film version of Ian Fleming's novel *Goldfinger.* Gert Fröbe as Auric Goldfinger, Harold Sakata as the henchman/caddy Oddjob, and Connery filmed the memorable golf scenes at Stoke Poges Golf Club outside of London.

The club now boasts a James Bond–themed bar. Ian Fleming was a golfer himself and a member of Royal St. George's Golf Club in Sandwich, Kent. He used this course as the inspiration for his fictional accounts of the game.

For all the respect James Bond received, Rodney Dangerfield got none playing the part of Al Czervik in *Caddyshack,* arguably the most hilarious golf movie of all time. Made in 1980, the film featured Chevy Chase, Bill Murray, Ted Knight, and an adorable gopher. Filmed at what is now known as Grande Oaks Golf Club, the action all takes place at mythical Bushwood Country Club, with a membership policy that reads "Some People Just Don't Belong."

Tin Cup, starring Kevin Costner as a seemingly washed-up club professional who qualifies for, and then contends in, the U.S. Open, was a huge hit when it came out in 1996.

In the 1970 smash hit *M*A*S*H,* surgeons Hawkeye (Donald Sutherland) and Trapper John (Elliott Gould) use a helipad as their practice tee. As a helicopter carrying a patient touches down, Trapper John declares: "I wish they wouldn't land those things here while we're playing golf."

For serious drama, there was Glenn Ford in *Follow the Sun* (1951), the inspirational story of Ben Hogan's comeback to win the 1950 U.S. Open after a near-fatal car crash in 1949. Starring Jim Caviezel, *Bobby Jones: Stroke of Genius* (2004) was another stirring biopic. It focused on the inner struggles of the only man ever to win the "Grand Slam" of four major championships in a single season, when he prevailed in the U.S. Open, U.S. Amateur, British Open, and British Amateur in 1930.

Dan Jenkins's riotous novel *Dead Solid Perfect* (1974) was adapted into a made-for-television movie with Randy Quaid, a five handicap, who needed twenty-six takes to pull off the "winning" shot.

Many golfers found inspiration in *The Legend of Bagger Vance* (2000) starring Matt Damon and Will Smith, or in the story of former caddy and twenty-year-old amateur Francis Ouimet's stunning victory in the 1913 U.S. Open as depicted by Matthew Knight in *The Greatest Game Ever Played* (2005).

5

THE BUNKER

The stately Allegheny Mountains bestow a cinematic backdrop on the long sojourn through West Virginia to a crossroads called White Sulphur Springs. Finally, the grand white Classical Revival Greenbrier resort and its three golf courses rise out of the mist.

Dating to 1778, the first cottages on the sixty-five-hundred-acre domain were designed by John H. B. Latrobe, son of famed United States Capitol architect Benjamin Latrobe. The original white hotel built in 1858 was later demolished and the iconic Greenbrier we know today was constructed around 1913.

Since then, luminaries such as Bing Crosby, Debbie Reynolds, and Princess Grace of Monaco, twenty-six U.S. presidents, countless members of Congress, and endless conventioneers have flocked to this retreat to play golf, dance the fox-trot, and take advantage of the mineral waters.

"Bunkers, if they be good bunkers, and bunkers of strong character, refuse to be disregarded, and insist on asserting themselves; they do not mind being avoided, but they decline to be ignored."
—*John L. Low,* Concerning Golf, *1903*

After World War II, celebrity decorator Dorothy Draper imprinted her signature bold style on the guest rooms and on ten majestic public spaces with black-and-white marble floors and large banana leaf prints accented by the West Virginia flower, rhododendron, in hot pink.

The Greenbrier's history as a golf destination emerged in the late 1940s, when three-time Masters winner Sam Snead returned to his hometown as head golf pro in the late 1940s. Between 1959 and 1962, the word *bunker*, normally thought of as a sand trap in these parts, took on another meaning.

As a new wing with additional luxury suites was added, construction workers labored under a shroud of secrecy while carving out a vast underground government relocation bunker sixty-four feet beneath the hotel. For more than thirty years, employees at the resort turned a blind eye to speculation concerning the intended use for the cavernous 112,000-square-foot space until writer Ted Gup outed the $86 million project in a 1992 *Washington Post* article. Now, in addition to a round of golf, guests can take a guided tour of this bunker of a different sort.

During the 1960s, dashing decorator Carleton Varney took over the Dorothy Draper firm and received a new assignment: to decorate the Greenbrier Golf Club, which includes Sam Snead's Tavern and Slammin' Sammy's Sports Bar.

To set the golf theme, Carleton began with a bright red plaid in the entrance of the clubhouse. "Of course golf is always linked with Scotland and, in turn, with plaid," he imparts. In order to maintain the overall experience of the entrance, he even used crimson Shannongrove Plaid wallpaper on the doors of the elevator as well as down the steps to the pro shop area.

"I knew Sam Snead, and I felt everything we did should be in homage to him," Carleton pronounces. For Sam Snead's Tavern, his vision was inspired by the location. The large golden-yellow dining area looks out over one of the resort's three golf courses to the mountains, so he used fabrics with trees. "We're near the Appalachians, and I related the design to the environment."

He also incorporated golf style into the club's interiors with four custom rug designs, which he begins by sketching on a yellow pad. "All the designs are

PREVIOUS PAGE: The Allegheny Mountains in West Virginia have been mystical since before the first cottages were built at The Greenbrier in 1778. ABOVE: Thanks to interior designer Dorothy Draper, the West Virginia state flower, a pink rhododendron, can be spotted on everything from the stationery to fleece vests and mugs at the resort. OPPOSITE: Soft spikes on a softer carpet.

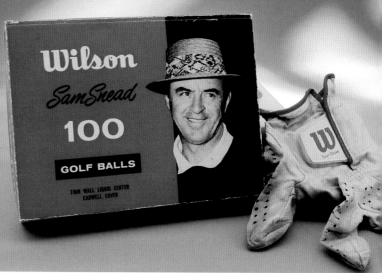

The Old White

- ⚑⚑ Restrooms
- △ Shelters
- ⚑ Anthony Cave Spring Water
- ★ Refreshment Stand

CLUB HOUSE
GOLF ACADEMY
DRIVING RANGE

The **Greenbrier**®
WHITE SULPHUR SPRINGS
WEST VIRGINIA 24986
www.greenbrier.com

Designed by
Charles Blair Macdonald
1914

CLOCKWISE FROM TOP LEFT: At the Greenbrier Sporting Club, an adjacent residential community, the Tom Fazio–designed course is aptly named The Snead. Many pieces of Sam Snead memorabilia are on display at The Greenbrier, with which he had a long association. The stately 6,500-acre White Sulphur Springs retreat was used as a 2,200-bed Army hospital during World War II. In the early 1960s, an $86-million emergency government underground bunker was installed and never used. It is now a tourist attraction. Golf architect Charles Blair Macdonald's circa-1914 Old White course remains a challenge and is a stop on the PGA Tour.

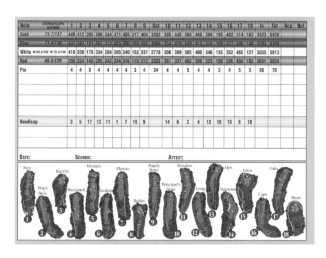

CLOCKWISE FROM TOP LEFT: Score card from The Old White Course at The Greenbrier. The golf club is tucked behind the resort's hotel. Carleton Varney designs everything touched by a guest, from the fabrics on the chairs to the china. Locally quarried fieldstone and sandstone were used for the Member's Lodge at the Greenbrier Sporting Club. The club is surrounded by the Tom Fazio–designed Snead Golf Course and dotted with private homes. Many of the residences are post and beam timber frame, built with the eco-friendly intention of protecting the natural surroundings at the base of Greenbrier Mountain and close to Howard's Creek. Golf aficionados from around the world arrive in grand style. The tee markers are an homage to Slammin' Sammy.

what is known as nondirectional because there are no lines—either vertical or horizontal," he explains. "This is important in a large space."

His imprint goes beyond fabric, wall coverings, and rugs. "Anything touched by a guest, we design," he states. This includes the china, glassware, linens, and menus. "Visually, everything should be tasteful. I don't believe in good and bad taste, only taste. You can't put your hand on taste; it's like fog. You can see it and feel it but you can't touch it."

To achieve golf style at home, Carleton recommends starting with a den or a family room. "Begin with the colors, such as green. There are so many shades of grass on a golf course," he notes. Instead of paint, he encourages the use of textured wall coverings. "If you have a large family room, think about having one wall paneled in wood. If you have a fireplace, use that wall." His preferences would include waxed pine or buttery beech wood.

"You can bring out the golf motif with lamps,"

OPPOSITE: When polished to perfection, old woods with colorful insets of painted weights provide understated style as a decorative accessory. CLOCKWISE FROM TOP LEFT: A wall-mounted shadow box with musical jazz instruments is a send-up to Snead as "The King of Swing." All the rugs, including the royal blue one with gold medallions and the green one with crossed clubs, were custom designed by Carleton Varney.

CLOCKWISE FROM LEFT: The Snead course at the Sporting Club has been designated a "Certified Audubon Cooperative Sanctuary." In order to achieve this certification, a number of environmental commitments are considered: wildlife and habitat management, chemical reduction, water conservation and quality, as well as outreach and education. Designer Carleton Varney's sketch for the Sam Snead restaurant. The various shades of green Varney used are an intentional reflection of the golf-inspired setting as seen in the completed room.

he continues, referring to several with golf motifs on display at The Greenbrier. "And think of the sky for inspiration. Paint the ceiling blue, and don't forget to add golf prints or art on the wall." Carlton urges cream linen for window treatments and a heavy tapestry patterned with golf scenes or equipment for the sofa. "There are so many golf fabrics, and I've used them many times."

Side chairs might be leather-covered wing chairs, with accent tables in pine or beech. Carleton is partial to using golf clubs as ornamental pieces. At The Greenbrier, the golf clubs are part of a seemingly endless treasure trove of Snead memorabilia on display.

Fondly referred to as "the King of Swing" for his perfectly synchronized stroke of the ball, Sam Snead, who died in May 2002 at age eighty-nine, won the Masters three times, the British Open once, and the PGA Championship four times, and had a record eighty-two victories on the PGA Tour, a record that still stands. As a send-up to his "swing," Carleton has a banjo and a trumpet displayed in a shadow box in the bar proclaiming "Sam Snead, the King of Swing."

"I never mastered chasing that little ball," exclaims Carleton, whose talents in interpreting golf style were clearly put to far better use off the course.

ABOVE and BELOW: A vivid red tartan called Shannongrove has been used throughout the bar area of the golf club. It is even echoed on the vests of the bartenders as they shake (rather than stir) a custom-made cocktail called The Slammer, made with two types of bourbon, Bols amaretto, and sloe gin.

OPPOSITE AND LEFT: Designer Carleton Varney suggests using lamps to punch up the golf motif in a room, such as this hand-painted ceramic one on a desk near the pro shop at The Greenbrier. Even the golf-style finials on the lamps contribute to the sense of detail.

"You can't put your hand on taste; it's like fog. You can see it and feel it but you can't touch it."
—Carleton Varney

OPPOSITE: The eighth hole on Old White, known as the Redan, is a facsimile of the fifteenth hole at North Berwick in Scotland. BELOW AND MIDDLE: The Redan has been described as a right-to-left running shot with the deepest bunker on the course just to the left of the green. BOTTOM: The first tee of the Greenbrier course. RIGHT: The Old White was designed by the legendary Charles Blair Macdonald.

THE OLD WHITE

On the three courses at The Greenbrier, golfers will find many "real" bunkers, including some designed by Canadian Charles Blair Macdonald (1855–1939). Known as the father of American Golf Architecture, Macdonald fell in love with golf at St. Andrews University in Scotland, where he fine-tuned his game at the Old Course under four-time British champion Old Tom Morris.

Striking out after college as a stockbroker in Chicago, Macdonald set aside golf for almost two decades until he designed, built, and founded the first golf course west of the Allegheny Mountains, the Chicago Golf Club, in 1892.

Instrumental in organizing the United States Golf Association in 1894, Macdonald won the first U.S. Amateur Championship the following year. He created his masterpiece—the National Golf Links of America on Long Island—in 1909. Many of the holes were replicas from St. Andrews, such as the Eden hole and the Road hole. Another was the Redan hole, a facsimile of the fifteenth hole at North Berwick in Scotland.

Macdonald, collaborating with Seth Raynor, reprised the Redan when asked to do the Old White Course in 1914 at The Greenbrier. The eighth hole on Old White is described as a right-to-left running shot with the deepest bunker on the course. It sits just to the left of the green.

6

THE FUNK FAMILY OF FLORIDA

When professional golfer Fred Funk began to envision his Florida dream home, his requirements were straightforward: a place for the family to spread out and be comfortable inside, and a putting green, a pool, and an expansive backyard outside.

His wife, Sharon, was responsible for the grander scheme of the architectural style, the interior atmosphere, and the spectacular surroundings.

The Funks found the perfect design collaborator. Sharon's brother, Rich Archer, a principal in Overland Partners, an architectural firm in San Antonio.

The result of their efforts is a collection of smaller buildings—a guest house, a children's pavilion, the main house, the garage and mudroom, and an entertainment house surrounding a glassy central living space along the majestic Intracoastal Waterway. The 9,722-square-foot residence has a contemporary

Tuscan aesthetic that derives a sense of warmth from earthy materials like stone and wood and old-world details like wrought iron, traditional millwork, and decorative tile.

A former golf coach at the University of Maryland, Fred achieved eight victories on the PGA Tour and now spends considerable time on the senior Champions Tour. "I feel like we're a big traveling circus out here on the Tour, whether it's the regular Tour or the Champions Tour, and we're a brotherhood," Fred said following his victory in the 2009 U.S. Senior Open at Crooked Stick Golf Club in Carmel, Indiana.

At home in Ponte Vedra, the Funk family, includ-

ing children Eric, Taylor, and Perri, gather most mornings for breakfast before Dad heads off to play a practice round. Sharon assembles the children for their homeschool program, which allows the close-knit family to spend more time together.

The kitchen, accented with stainless-steel appliances, was designed to have an old-world atmosphere. To offset an absence of natural illumination, a skylight was incorporated, and mono-point track spot beams focus on the stained concrete center island. "Downlighting an island creates a kind of hearth-like, illuminated center around which people tend to cluster, similar to gathering around a fire. It's very communal," says Kin Bolz, who served as project manager and now oversees her own firm.

"The kitchen also was designed to have views of the pool area to keep an eye on the children," adds Kin, who has since struck out on her own. The breakfast area, where Fred reads the morning papers, is

PAGE 85: A private putting green offers a place to practice as well as a sanctuary for family. **OPPOSITE and ABOVE LEFT:** The front door was designed to provide privacy from the outside and add light in the entry area. **ABOVE RIGHT:** Sharon and Fred Funk enjoy mornings in their kitchen, where the table was intentionally raised from the living room to afford a view of the yard and waterway beyond.

THE FUNK FAMILY OF FLORIDA | 87

raised from the living room for a view to the yard and the water beyond.

In the neighboring great room and on the patio outside, Kota Blue honed limestone flooring from India has been used for continuity between the home's interior and its exterior. Around the fireplace partition in the great room, guests discover an ever-changing decor as Sharon acquires new pieces in her travels. Yet, amid the collection of striking pieces from Belgium, Kentucky, and Tennessee, there is a genuine sense of casual living, which suits the continuous flow of children, dogs, and friends.

Working toward an Italian minimalist style advocated by designer John Saladino, Sharon created a file with photos of his work and pored through his books. The inside and outside seating, ottomans, tables, light fixtures, and artwork are distinguished as four-sided figures, triangles, and oblong objets d'art according to the Saladino way. While accompanying Fred around the world for golf tournaments, Sharon found time to visit antiques shops for unusual pieces of furniture and to scour salvage warehouses for large architectural accents that she could trans-

late into Saladino's philosophy of using furnishings as geometry. An ornate old stone *F* mounted on the wall of the entrance courtyard is one such touch.

"She had an understanding of what she wanted and a strong sense of style," says decorator Karen Orr of Florida Home and Design, who worked with Sharon to accomplish her vision.

A major ingredient of this approach is an intentional blurring of the lines between inside and out. While at home, the Funks frequently entertain, and the intimate dining room overlooking the courtyard and guest pavilion offers the ideal space for a small dinner party. A two-sided raised-hearth fireplace can be seen at table height along one wall and on floor height on the opposite side in the living room. Stone walls with chunky timber lintels broaden the Tuscan atmosphere.

An expanse of intersliding glass doors connects the great room to a covered back porch, which can be opened for large gatherings, such as the Funks' party during the The Players championship each May. Integrated sliding screen panels from Phantom Screens were added at the perimeter of the porch between the columns.

Beyond, the house's expansive backyard transitions into an extension of the main living area. There, Fred's wishes for a dream house have come true: a lap pool, a fire pit with trellis, and, of course, the ultimate in golf style—a practice putting green for the Funk family of Florida.

PREVIOUS PAGES: Sharon Funk chose an Italian minimalist style for the home. **LEFT:** The large black painted chest was found while traveling. **OPPOSITE:** When the Mediterranean clay roof tiles arrived in the wrong color, Sharon pulled out her paints to give them the right muted look. The Italian feel continues outside with stone accents poolside.

LEFT: As an accent piece, a sculpted torso befits the Italian atmosphere. The tall candlesticks behind the sculpture and the even taller wrought-iron candelabra add an Italian ecclesiastical element to the space. **ABOVE:** There's a putter available for every member of the Funk family as well as for guests. The exterior stone wall is a rectangular ashlar cut, Tennessee Crab Orchard. **BELOW:** Fred plays at the nearby TPC Sawgrass course, depicted here by artist Adriano Manocchia. The artist says, "On a course like Sawgrass, morning brings long shadows that stretch across the greens and the sparkle of fresh dew on the grass."

CLOCKWISE FROM TOP LEFT: An ornamental stone *F* at the entrance informs guests they've reached the right place. In the dining room, the two-sided raised fireplace is table height so that guests can view it. The wrought-iron doors on the wine closet were custom designed. Fred Funk competes on both the PGA Tour and the senior Champions Tour for players fifty and over. The Funk family home was designed by Sharon's brother Rick Archer to portray a Tuscan ambiance.

THE FUNK FAMILY OF FLORIDA | 93

7

Papering the House

Whether making a strong statement with vivid stripes or opting for a soft tone with a subtle strié, a burnished leather look, or formal damask, adding wallpaper of any design to an entryway, room, or wall bestows character to a space.

Golf lovers can also choose from wall coverings with a golf theme drawn from iconic images of the game— golf clubs, putters, balls, or memorable landscapes.

When considering color, golf style frequently incorporates hues of green. "Most country clubs use green, which is funny since you are usually looking out at green fairways," says Stacy Senior Allan of Thibaut Wallpaper and Fabrics. "But that's what this is all about: bringing the outside in to draw attention to the interiors."

To capture this subject matter, Thibaut introduced the Castle Pine Collection with "Golf" in six

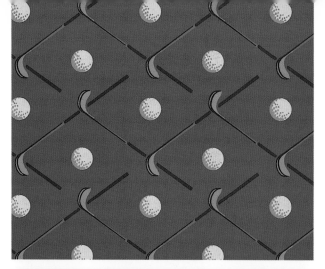

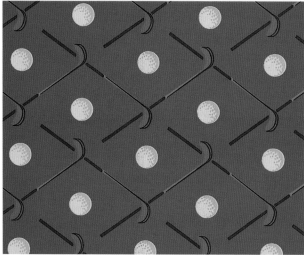

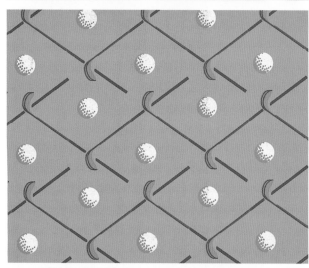

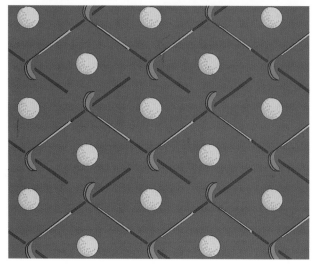

traditional colors (green, red, brown, beige, black, and gold) in wallpaper and coordinating fabrics. Established in 1886, the firm is noted for its classic creations and for its use of handsome palettes without elaborate names for colors. The color is simply called green, not emerald or spruce.

"A home office or a study is the first place I'd think to use the smaller pattern called 'Miniature Golf,'" Stacy says, "or for larger homes, a library or a game room." The pattern would also suit a boy's bedroom or even a golf-loving girl's bedroom because a small pattern can easily work in a large room. "It's a simple graphic design, and from far away it almost looks like a trellis and becomes a background pattern," she explains.

The reverse technique, using a big print in a small space, also works, according to Stacy: "Large prints can work in a small room. It's something to look at, like little pictures on the wall." This is particularly useful for small rooms such as a powder room with no windows.

To create an outsize landscape print, Thibaut art director Lori Reagle and other designers studied historical renderings of golf. They envisioned an "art print" sentiment. Utilizing the same basic background colors, a series of medallions and hexagon shapes showcases vistas of golf courses from around the world, conjuring up memories of Pebble Beach, Augusta National, Shinnecock Hills, and St. Andrews.

PREVIOUS PAGE AND LEFT: The four colorways of this line of wall coverings can be coordinated with a companion pattern as well as with fabrics. **OPPOSITE:** When considering wall coverings for a bath or powder room, there are numerous choices in both paper and vinyl finishes. Some designers suggest using a small print for such spaces. A decorative towel rail completes the attention to details.

PINE NEEDLES

At Pine Needles Resort, tucked in among the tower-ing loblolly and longleaf pines along Midland Road in Southern Pines, North Carolina, interior design-ers Pam Hill and Susan Brown of the Village Design Group evoked a cozy golf ambiance with the strate-gic use of wallpaper. Not wanting to overpower guests with too much golf, they began with three different room palettes of buff, teal, or red against a backdrop of knotty pine walls. Surrounded by golf art and golf lamps, guests get the feeling of "Hey, we're in Pinehurst," says Pam, who wanted to main-tain a uniform feel in the lodge without a cookie-cutter footprint in every room. "We staggered the designs down the hall." She punched up the individ-uality of the rooms by installing golf-themed wall-paper from Waverly, Schumacher, and Seabrook in the bathrooms.

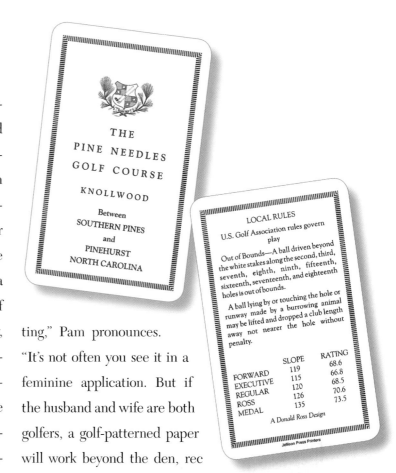

For wall covering ideas, Pam suggests the sample books of Imperial, Blonder, and Brewster. "Typically anything with golf is going to reflect a masculine set-ting," Pam pronounces. "It's not often you see it in a feminine application. But if the husband and wife are both golfers, a golf-patterned paper will work beyond the den, rec room, and other settings."

As the resort expanded, Peggy Bell Miller, daugh-ter of owner/octogenarian Peggy Kirk Bell, a found-ing member of the LPGA, took over some of the decorating duties. To update existing rooms and fluff up additional accommodations, she began by explor-ing local shops for golf-associated textiles and hired local seamstresses to make pillows and shams out of them. For lighting, she searched the Internet and found pinecone lamps and golf-themed light fixtures at www.shadesoflight.com. Wanting to also patron-ize local retail shops, Peggy discovered additional furniture pieces at Mid-State Furniture in nearby Carthage.

OPPOSITE: Just across Midland Road, the striking Mid Pines resort offers another Donald Ross–designed course.
FOLLOWING PAGES: Pine Needles dates to 1927, when the Tufts family, developers of the Village of Pinehurst and the Carolina Hotel, added yet another holding and asked Donald Ross to design the course. The reception room in the lodge presents several intimate seating areas for a home-away-from-home living room impression.

PINE NEEDLES LODGE & GOLF CLUB

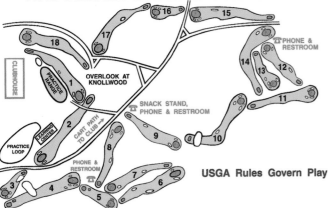

USGA Rules Govern Play

IN CASE OF EMERGENCY DIAL 2227 ON PHONES LOCATED ON HOLES
#5 & #9 AND BETWEEN THE 12TH AND 14TH GREENS.
www.pineneedles-midpines.com

CLOCKWISE FROM TOP LEFT: For the rooms in the lodge at Pine Needles, Peggy Bell Miller purchased golf fabrics for pillows and shams. For lighting, she found an elegant golf club–adorned lamp and two lamps of golfers taking practice shots (below and bottom left). Warren and Peggy Kirk Bell, a founding member of the LPGA who traveled the pro circuit flying her own airplane. She sold the plane and used the proceeds to build a pool at Pine Needles.

ABOVE: The main lodge at Pine Needles overlooks an all-weather practice shelter built to maintain the rustic atmosphere. The individual nooks for the golfers are set off by barn doors. **BELOW:** In the area surrounding the Village of Pinehurst, there are dozens of options for all levels of play for golfers from a simple 9 hole pitch and putt course to a four-star challenge of 18 holes. **LEFT:** A golfer's towel, intended to hang on the bag while playing, doubles as a hand towel that perfectly complements the blue tones of the bathroom wall covering.

GOLF COURSES OF THE U.S. OPEN

100

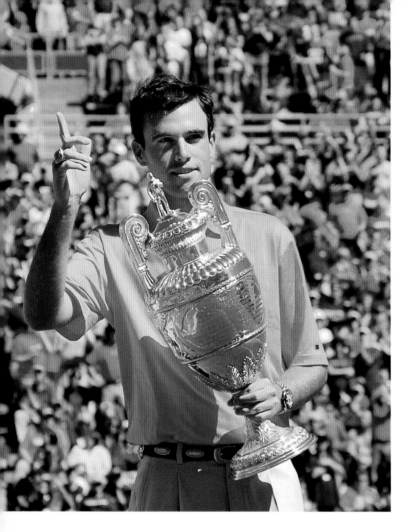

PREVIOUS PAGES: Achieving golf style can be as simple as adding a few pillows and an elegant piece of sculpture to an otherwise ordinary space. **ABOVE and BELOW:** After winning the British Amateur title in 2007, Drew Weaver was honored by his classmates at Virginia Tech as Male Athlete-of-the-Year. Drew was within one hundred yards of the April 16, 2007, event that took the lives of thirty-two other students and faculty at Tech and now dedicates each round he plays as a professional to their memory.

HIGH POINTS

Cathy Weaver and John Weaver also shop in their area of North Carolina for furnishings to indulge an ever-growing interest in the sport and an expanding array of trophies won by their son, Drew.

The Weavers have updated their 1970s brick rambler three times since 1981. Each time, they made changes as Drew's collection of golf memorabilia and trophies, including the gold medal from the 2007 British Amateur Championship, continued to grow.

"John has always loved golf, but once Drew was soundly headed in that direction, I moved other decorative items, such as porcelain birds, out of the family room and simply consolidated the golf awards in one room," Cathy Weaver recalls.

"We first filled the built-in cabinets in the great room with trophies, and that just became too cluttered," says Cathy, a public relations consultant. "Finally, we removed a secretary and replaced it with a nice trophy case, which is now home to the most prized and most current trophies."

The original master bedroom became Drew's room when a new master suite was added to the house in 2002. "It made a lot of sense to move Drew into this room because of the three closets," Cathy explains.

John Weaver, who has a full schedule as a family physician, worked on weekends sketching designs for shelves and drawers, and he also added lighting inside the closets. "He was a home-improvement guy before they invented it on TV," Cathy jokes. "I'd absolutely never think about measuring how much hanging space I need in a closet and then making it fit, but John does."

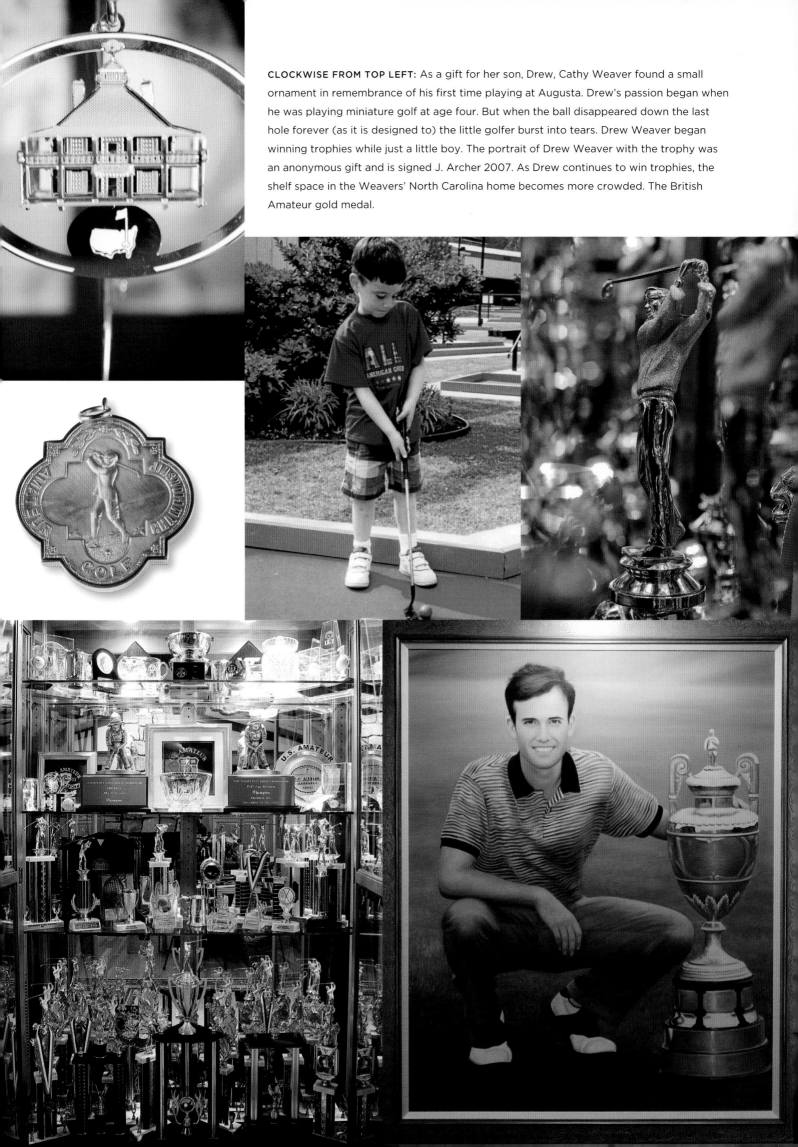

CLOCKWISE FROM TOP LEFT: As a gift for her son, Drew, Cathy Weaver found a small ornament in remembrance of his first time playing at Augusta. Drew's passion began when he was playing miniature golf at age four. But when the ball disappeared down the last hole forever (as it is designed to) the little golfer burst into tears. Drew Weaver began winning trophies while just a little boy. The portrait of Drew Weaver with the trophy was an anonymous gift and is signed J. Archer 2007. As Drew continues to win trophies, the shelf space in the Weavers' North Carolina home becomes more crowded. The British Amateur gold medal.

CLOCKWISE FROM TOP LEFT: John Weaver, a physician, designed the shelf space for son Drew's golf-inspired room. The Weavers have collected a number of pillows from memorable tournaments. Cathy Weaver has a knack for finding all kinds of clever golf desk, dining table accessories, and this display rack made to hold the iconic short golf scoring pencils collected while traveling. As her son's biggest fan, Cathy sends out e-mail updates from each tournament to friends and family now known as "Drew's Crew." At one tournament she noted with good humor: "Good morning. Not enough sleep last night. At 3:20 A.M., I woke up to hear someone yell 'FORE' and then hit a ball down our hall in the motel. Something tells me he didn't make the cut!"

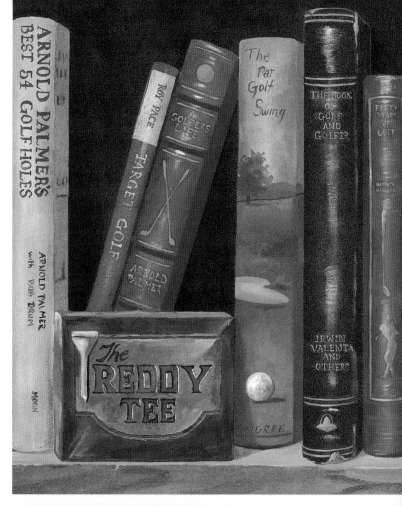

RIGHT, ABOVE and BELOW: Using a wallpaper border lifted a young man's bedroom out of the ordinary and crystallized the golf theme. Living in the furniture capital of High Point, North Carolina, made it effortless to furnish the young golfer's room with a painted dresser and other details such as the golf-ball finial.

"Drew likes to group his sweaters by style [cashmere, cable, V-neck, lightweight for spring, heavy for winter] and the lighting really helps him make the best use of all the shelves—top to bottom."

The young golfer's room is a compilation of pieces from the furniture capital of the world—his hometown, High Point. Cathy collects pillows from various golf tournaments and uses them as accent pieces throughout the house; she also hunts for golf-related desktop sit-abouts for Drew and John. On one hunt to the outlet stores she discovered Drew's bed and dresser for $225. "It's black, so it's pretty forgiving when it comes to damage. It's simple to disguise blemishes on black furniture."

The bedding reflects a young golfer's taste in classic clothing. "We wanted colors that looked like Drew," Cathy says. "Plus, if you use dark blues, dark greens, deep burgundy and reds, and rich taupe, it will go with any man's golf memorabilia." A plaid comforter with a light blue chambray contrast, oxford-cloth striped sheets (from T.J. Maxx), and lots of pillows illustrate the scheme.

And to complete the idea, she papered the room with a golf-related border (found online at www .usawallpaper.com). "It's one of the more detailed and classic golf-themed wallpapers," Cathy concludes. And if Drew keeps winning tournaments, the Weavers will be adding on to their home yet again. And then they will not only have more walls to cover; they just might be building more shelves to hold more trophies.

8

CYMRU A GOLFF

W hen it comes to golf in far-off places, one of the best kept secrets is Wales, with its historic, uncrowded courses and handsome examples of style and design on and off the green.

One prominent recurring design is "Y Ddraig Goch"—the red dragon—which dates to 1485, when it was first used on a flag by Henry VII. This mascot, fondly referred to as Merlin, is now seen on everything from taxi doors to ties and teacups. One of the finest examples of red dragon–themed design can be found on fourteen hundred luscious acres just outside Cardiff, Wales, at the posh Celtic Manor resort.

A giant hand-carved pair of these symbolic creatures greets guests in the atrium of the resort's main hotel. Weighing in at one ton each and wrapped around two massive columns, they were

The knight brandished his bright blade, and it seemed sharper than ever, his hands even stronger. He smote the crested head with a blow so mighty that the dragon reared up like a hundred raging lions.

—Saint George and the Dragon, *as adapted by Margaret Hodges from Edmund Spenser's* The Faerie Queene

commissioned by owner Sir Terence Matthews and created by Frank Triggs at his studio, Woodforms, in Gwern-y-Brenin in mid-Wales.

"I wanted to create something of sufficient power to hold its own in a large space like this," Frank says. "Technically, they were much more difficult than a freestanding sculpture because they had to be exactly the right size to cling to the columns."

It is customary for golfers to pat the smiling dragon for good luck as they head out to play on one of the three championship courses. Upon closer inspection, however, golfers will discover that while the outgoing dragon is smiling, the returning dragon is frowning.

No doubt Sir Terence, a telecommunications entrepreneur and Wales's first billionaire, has patted the dragon a few times himself. His good fortune is responsible for Celtic Manor's £16 million Twenty Ten course, the first in history to be designed specifically to host the Ryder Cup in 2010.

Only a very occasional golfer, Sir Terence first met the golf course architect Robert Trent Jones in 1980 at Jones's Fort Lauderdale base, the Coral Ridge Country Club. The designer eventually put him in touch with people at the European Tour involved in site selections for future Cup competitions. Jones also designed the first golf course at Celtic Manor, called "the Roman Road" because the remnants of

that ancient trail are still visible from the course.

"It's no longer just a golf tournament," Sir Terence says of the Ryder Cup. "It's the third largest spectator event on the planet, after the World Cup and the Super Bowl. And when we told European Tour officials we were going to build a course specifically designed for a match play event like the Ryder Cup, we definitely got their attention."

Indeed, the dramatic design of the Twenty Ten Clubhouse grabs the attention of visiting golfers and nongolfers alike. Partially clad in rendered masonry, with a slate-covered pitched roof, the longhouse frame is Scotch pine with western red cedar. "We would describe the appearance as traditional lodge accommodation with perimeter viewing balconies," says Cardiff-based architect Richard Thomas of HLN Architects.

Richard defines the key word throughout as *luxury*. With thousands of visitors coming from around the world for the Ryder Cup, the property was designed to accommodate an influx of traffic and spectators while maintaining the clubby atmosphere of an intimate setting. This includes a cherry-paneled members' lounge and imposing oak doors throughout. The spacious open Spike Bar on the lower ground floor combines old and new aesthetics with traditional exposed barn timber frames and stone walls

PAGE 111: Golfing in Wales has taken on a new dimension since the country hosted the 2010 Ryder Cup. **OPPOSITE:** Sir Terence Matthews, the first billionaire in Wales, developed Celtic Manor Resort, which now has three dynamic courses, including the £16 million Twenty Ten course. **ABOVE:** One of a pair of hand-carved dragons that loom large in the atrium at Celtic Manor.

CLOCKWISE FROM LEFT: A well-known round red Royal Mail box adds a subtle touch of Great Britain in the contemporary atrium lobby at Celtic Manor. As golfers approach the eighteenth hole on the Twenty Ten course, the clubhouse looms in the distance across a pond. Designed by Cardiff-based architect Richard Thomas of HLN Architects, the pitched roof of the clubhouse is slate with a longhouse frame in Scotch pine and western red cedar. "The design evolved in consideration of U.K. building styles," the architect explains, adding that the ultimate goal was luxury.

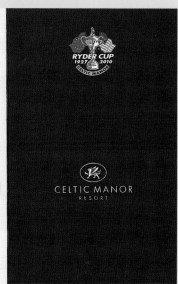

CELTIC MANOR COURSES

The Roman Road—designed by Robert Trent Jones
The Twenty Ten—designed by Ross McMurray of European Golf Design
The Montgomerie—designed by Scottish-born golfer Colin Montgomerie

CLOCKWISE FROM TOP LEFT: Fondly referred to as Merlin, Y Ddraig Goch, the red dragon, can been seen on everything from taxi doors to ties. This topiary at the Twenty Ten course will remain long after the year changes. It has been said that Celtic Manor is where dragons play. Some golfers might even encounter one on the golf course, such as this very whimsical ball marker.

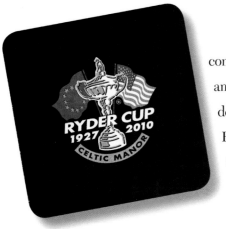

complemented by glass and steel balconies. The design of the adjacent Rafters restaurant also incorporates dramatic timber beams.

As players approach the eighteenth hole, the clubhouse can be seen in the distance across a pond. A guidebook to the course cautions all who dare to play this hole that "the green is further defended by a pair of sizable bunkers that can easily snare anything too ambitious and, at the last hole, in front of a huge crowd, any player would be keen to avoid them."

STAR GAZING

Among the crowd of spectators at golf tournaments in Wales, a keen-eyed star gazer might spot singer Charlotte Church, who is often behind the gallery ropes with her children. Star gazing on the course is almost as much of a sport as the game itself.

Leading the pack from a golfer's point view would be 1991 Masters champion Welshman Ian "Woosie" Woosnam, captain of the winning 2006 Ryder Cup European team. Woosie's home course is Llanymynech in Wales, where three of the eighteen holes are actually located in England. "On the fourth you tee off in Wales, putt out in England, and return to Wales three holes later," he says.

Other golfing glitterati from Wales: stage star Jonathan Pryce, Rhys Ifans from the movie *Notting Hill,*

writer Ken Follett, Matthew Rhys (better known as Kevin Walker on the television drama *Brothers and Sisters*), *Access Hollywood* reporter Tim Vincent, actress Jane Seymour, rock legend Meat Loaf, and Academy Award winner Catherine Zeta-Jones.

Catherine Zeta-Jones and her husband, actor Michael Douglas, are members at Langland Bay Golf Club, which was founded in 1904 in the charming village of Mumbles. Fellow member/designer Gil Lewis did a recent renovation of the clubhouse here, offering a fresh interpretation of the dated, dark room. "Looking out the windows from the clubhouse, I could see the sea and the sand beyond," she says. Her approach of considering the exterior before finalizing the interior design could easily be translated for home decor. "I took away the ancient dark paneling and made the room brighter with bleached flooring and soft sea-foam fabrics."

Gil's elegant makeover was complete in time for the club's centenary celebrations, topped off by a visit by the Duke of York. An enthusiastic golfer, Prince Andrew also has played at the various venues of the British Open.

When he's in his homeland, the great Welsh actor Anthony Hopkins plays at Pyle & Kenfig, or at the breathtaking and historic Royal Porthcawl adjacent to

Ryder Cup
Cocktails

Western Comfort £7.25
Bourbon, Grand Marnier and Ginger Ale on Ice

Happy Gilmore £7.25
Kahlua, Frangelico and Crème de Cocoa with a sprinkle of Cinnamon

Fresh Cut Fairway £7.25
White Rum, Peach Schnapps, Apple Schnapps and Orange Juice

Valhalla Ryder Cup Martini £7.25
Bourbon, Amaretto and Pineapple Juice

ABOVE: At Celtic Manor, guests from around the world can enjoy custom-made cocktails such as the Western Comfort combination of bourbon, Grand Marnier, and ginger ale or, as a send-up to the 2008 international team competition held in Kentucky, a Valhalla Ryder Cup Martini, a lively concoction of bourbon, Amaretto, and pineapple juice.

CLOCKWISE FROM TOP LEFT: Welsh native and Academy Award–winner Catherine Zeta-Jones celebrates a great moment on the course during the celebrity charity golf tournament at Celtic Manor. Founded in 1904, Langland Bay Golf Club has members including actors Catherine Zeta-Jones and her husband, Michael Douglas. Interior designer Gil Lewis took her inspiration from the views of the distant sea in bringing the pale blue colors inside for the renovations of the formerly dark-paneled clubhouse at Langland Bay. As at most clubs, members are urged to smooth the bunkers, to not take practice swings on the tee, and to replace the divots.

LANGLAND BAY GOLF CLUB

Established 1904

LANGLAND BAY GOLF CLUB

- RULES & ETIQUETTE REGARDING SLOW PLAY MUST BE OBSERVED
- KEEP TROLLEYS OFF TEES & GREENS
- SMOOTH BUNKERS AFTER PLAY
- REPAIR PITCH MARKS ON GREENS
- REPLACE DIVOTS
- DO NOT TAKE PRACTICE SWINGS ON TEES

29/9/08
SHEET
ANCHOR
SOCIETY
1.45 - 2.45

OPPOSITE: The Matthews Cup for the Twenty Ten club championship remains on display throughout the year. **CLOCKWISE FROM TOP LEFT:** In the members' lounge at the Twenty Ten club, a small collection of books offers a selection on history, statistics, and the ever-popular genre of how-to. When not in use for large international tournaments, the Twenty Ten is a private club. It is the first facility built to host a Ryder Cup. Old exposed barn timber frames and stone walls merge with glass in The Rafters restaurant. Merlin brings magic and mystery everywhere he goes.

PREVIOUS PAGES: Golfers must use a trolley for their clubs at the breathtaking and historic (1891) Royal Porthcawl classic links course adjacent to the Bristol Channel. **ABOVE:** In order for a golf club to use the "Royal" prefix, the honor must be bestowed by a member of the British royal family. Royal Porthcawl received this distinction from King Edward VII in 1909. Many of the historic clubs have a men's-only lounge. **OPPOSITE, TOP TO BOTTOM:** A weathervane atop an outbuilding at the Langland Bay Golf Club outside the charming Welsh village of Mumbles advises golfers of the prevailing winds coming off the nearby Swansea Bay. For golfing bibliophiles visiting Wales, the town of Hay-on-Wye is a must-stop. Bilingual signs along the winding rural roads direct visitors to the town of books.

the Bristol Channel, a classic links venue that dates from 1891. A young Tiger Woods played there on the losing American team in the 1995 Walker Cup, an international match play competition between amateurs from the United States and the British Isles. The bib Woods's caddy used that week still hangs in the tiny pro shop.

BOOKED UP

On the well-stocked shelves of the village of Hay-on-Wye's bookshops, golfing bibliophiles discover the treasures offered by more than thirty dealers of secondhand and antique books.

One such cherished book might be *On Golf*, written by the late Bernard Darwin, a top British amateur golfer turned columnist for *The Times* and *Country Life* magazine, and grandson of naturalist Charles Darwin, who along with his wife, Emma, raised Bernard. While strolling along Castle and Lion Street in Hay-on-Wye (Y Gelli Gandryll in Welsh), fans of Darwin's should also seek out some of his other books, which include: *The Golf Courses of the British Isles* (with artwork by Harry Rountree) and *Golf Is My Game*.

Or, one might come across a certain tale about Saint George and the Dragon in the stacks. "When the tale ended the king said, "Never did living man sail through such a sea of deadly dangers. Since you are now safely come to shore, stay here and live happily ever after. You have earned your rest."

9

PRETTY IN PINK AND GREEN: AUGUSTA AND THE MASTERS

Every April like clockwork, golf pilgrims make their way to the bustling Georgia town of Augusta for a colorful feast of lush landscape, sumptuous food, preppy fashion, and riveting competition.

It all begins as a spectacular pink and green array of foliage bursts forth in the paradise known as Augusta National Golf Club. More than 80,000 plants in 250 varieties are front and center for the most revered competition in golf . . . The Masters.

A private golf club was formed in 1930 when champion golfer Robert "Bobby" T. Jones and investment banker Clifford Roberts purchased the property for $70,000 and later sold memberships in what they referred to as a "national" club. They hired designer Alister MacKenzie to execute their vision of undulating putting surfaces and relatively few bunkers.

FOLIAGE

The 365-acre former indigo plantation was acquired in 1857 by a horticultural devotee, the Belgian baron Louis Mathieu Edouard Berckmans. The following year, Berckmans and his son founded Fruitland Nurseries on the site; many of their trees and shrubs—especially the vibrant azaleas—are still on display.

An allée of sixty-one magnolia trees planted 150 years ago leads to the circa 1854 clubhouse, which is regarded as the first cement house constructed in the South. In front of the clubhouse, a flower bed in the shape of the Masters logo (a United States map with a flagstick) blooms with yellow pansies in the spring, marigolds in the summer, and chrysanthemums in the fall.

A huge oak tree (*Quercus virginiana*) near the clubhouse, a popular meeting point for spectators, was planted around the same time the building went up. A hundred-year-old loblolly pine (*Pinus taeda*) near hole No. 17 was affectionately christened "the Eisenhower Tree" in honor of former president Dwight Eisenhower. An avid golfer, Ike frequently hit errant balls into the tree; and at one time he even proposed that the so-called obstacle be cut down. He was politely overruled.

Each hole on the course is named for a variety of Southern vegetation: tea olive, pink dogwood, flowering peach, flowering crab apple, magnolia, juniper, pampas, yellow jasmine, Carolina cherry, camellia, white dogwood, golden bell, azalea (of which there are thirty eye-popping varieties), firethorn, redbud, nandina, holly, and the somewhat exotic China fir.

FOOD

During the week of the Masters, spectators can treat themselves in the gift shop to the highly recognizable verdant green cap, pastel-colored tote bags, golf shirts, and perhaps a copy of the Junior League of Augusta's cookbook *Par 3: Tea-Time at the Masters*, featuring a delicious Pink Pound Cake (which perfectly matches all the surrounding pink flowers).

The $1.50 pimiento cheese sandwich is a lunchtime specialty and Southern staple, and signature sandwich. It comes on ordinary white bread with mayonnaise and is sealed in a green Baggie.

Another mealtime ritual happens in Augusta on Tuesday evening during the week of the tournament, when an exclusive Champion's Dinner is hosted by the defending champion for previous winners and select honorary guests, mostly members of the club.

The defending champion selects the menu, which often includes regional or international cuisine. The German-type Wiener schnitzel and spaetzle with Black Forest cake for dessert was chosen by Bernhard Langer in 1986. The 2000 champion, Fiji native Vijay Singh, offered seafood *tom kah,* chicken Panang curry,

PREVIOUS PAGE: The green jacket of Augusta National Golf Club members and Masters champions is the most famous piece of clothing in menswear. **OPPOSITE, CLOCKWISE FROM TOP LEFT:** Every shade of green can be seen during Masters week. Flags add to the international flair. The real reason President Eisenhower didn't want anyone to ask about his score at Augusta is because of his well-known errant balls. A tree on the property was named in his honor; when he proposed chopping down the obstacle, he was politely overruled. Even the popular "pimento" cheese sandwiches are wrapped in green. The course as depicted by Sam Ingwersen.

NAME OF GOLF HOLES

1 ....Tea Olive
2 ....Pink Dogwood
3 ....Flowering Peach
4 ....Flowering Crabapple
5 ....Magnolia
6 ....Juniper
7 ....Pampas
8 ....Yellow Jasmine
9 ....Carolina Cherry
10 ....Camellia
11 ....White Dogwood
12 ....Golden Bell
13 ....Azalea
14 ....Chinese Fir
15 ....Fire Thorn
16 ....Red Bud
17 ....Nandina
18 ....Holly

AUGUSTA NATIONAL GOLF CLUB

BELOW: Each hole on the Augusta National course celebrates Southern horticulture, from the iconic dogwood to the holly to the front-and-center azalea. **RIGHT:** Tom Watson. **OPPOSITE:** Accented with a bed of yellow pansies, the circa-1854 clubhouse has been frequently referred to as the first cement house constructed in the South.

Well, it's springtime in the valley on Magnolia Lane

It's the Augusta National and the master of the game

Who'll wear that green coat on Sunday afternoon?

Who'll walk that eighteenth fairway singing this tune?

Augusta, your dogwoods and pines

They play on my mind like a song

Augusta, it's you that I love

And it's you that I'll miss when I'm gone.

It's Watson, Byron Nelson, Demaret, Player and Snead

It's Amen Corner and it's Hogan's perfect swing

It's Sarazen's double eagle at the fifteenth in thirty-five

And the spirit of Clifford Roberts that keeps it alive

Augusta, your dogwoods and pines

They play on my mind like a song

Augusta, it's you that I love

And it's you that I miss when I'm gone

It's the legions of Arnie's army and the Golden Bear's throngs

And the wooden-shafted legend of Bobby Jones.

—from "Augusta," by Dave Loggins, inspired by a visit to Augusta in 1980

baked sea scallops with garlic sauce, rack of lamb with yellow *kari* sauce, and baked filet of Chilean sea bass with three-flavor chili sauce. He finished the meal with lychee sorbet.

The celebrations continue on Wednesday evening, when the Golf Writers Association of America gathers at the Savannah Rapids Pavilion. Situated five miles from the course on a beautiful eighty-foot bluff, the site overlooks the Savannah River and the Augusta Canal. Held in honor of leading players, officials, and journalists, the event, attended by three hundred plus guests, begins with a cocktail hour, followed by dinner and awards in the White Oak Room. Five types of wine from the Cosentino vineyards are offered up during the four-course meal courtesy of Mitch Cosentino, a devoted follower of the sport. Player of the year honorees have included nine-time winner Tiger Woods, Padraig Harrington, Fred Couples, Annika Sorenstam, Jay Haas, and Lee Trevino.

The bestowing of the Ben Hogan award from the golf writers always brings tears of joy, as it honors someone involved in the sport (player, caddy, or journalist) who has overcome a serious illness or has played despite a physical handicap. In 2009, Erik Compton, a native of South Florida who has had two heart transplants, mesmerized the crowd with his memory of waking up from his last surgery the year before and wondering if he would ever be able to play again. Within a year, he was breaking par again and hoping to earn full-time playing privileges on the PGA Tour.

ABOVE: A ticket to the Masters is certainly the most coveted in golf. **LEFT:** Irishman Padraig Harrington and his son, Patrick, during the Par 3 contest traditionally held on Wednesday during Masters week. **OPPOSITE:** While the green jacket gets all the fanfare at the Masters, the winner is also awarded a sterling-silver trophy that consists of nine hundred pieces of silver in the form of the clubhouse, $1.35 million in first-place money, and a gold medal.

PINK POUND CAKE

Serves 12

3 cups all-purpose flour
1 teaspoon baking powder
½ teaspoon salt
4 eggs
1 cup milk
1 teaspoon vanilla extract
1 cup (2 sticks) margarine, softened
2 cups sugar
1 (3-ounce) box strawberry gelatin
1 (10-ounce) package frozen strawberries in syrup, thawed

Preheat the oven to 325 degrees.

Mix the flour, baking powder and salt together. Mix the eggs, milk and vanilla in a bowl. Beat the margarine, sugar and gelatin in a large bowl until light and fluffy. Stir in the dry ingredients alternately with the milk mixture. Fold in the strawberries. Pour into a nonstick Bundt pan.

Bake for 70 to 75 minutes or until a wooden pick inserted in the center comes out clean. Cool in the pan for 10 minutes. Remove to a wire rack to cool completely.

—*Par 3: Tea-Time at the Masters,* Junior League of Augusta, Georgia

FASHION

On the golf course, spectators clad in sherbet-colored Lilly Pulitzers view the action on one of the world's most photogenic courses. The Masters ends with the new champion being invited to Butler Cabin on Sunday evening to be presented with the coveted green jacket by the previous year's winner.

Arguably the most famous fashion statement in all of sports, the jacket is crafted at the Hamilton Tailoring company in Ohio, from two and a half yards of tropical-weight wool from the Forstmann Company of Georgia. The green color was chosen to be reminiscent of the fairways, and in the late 1930s the first sample swatches came from the Hunt and Winterbotham mill in West England. The color has since been standardized to Pantone 342, which is also used by Ohio University, Kenya, and Turkmenistan.

Intended to be worn exclusively by members of Augusta National beginning in 1937, a jacket has been given to the winner of the Masters since 1949. Sam Snead was the first recipient. His jacket, now on display at The Greenbrier, is actually a replacement. The original was stolen, and Sam waited years before he got up the nerve to ask for another; instead he wore a two-inch-shorter version belonging to Bobby Jones.

Jack Nicklaus was only twenty-four when he won his first green jacket in 1963; yet it was not until thirty-five years later that he got one of his own. At first he wore one on loan from 1948 Republican presidential nominee Thomas Dewey. He later had a green jacket made on his own, but the color didn't quite match. Then he borrowed another one. As an honorary member of Augusta National, he mentioned the oversight to a fellow member in 1998 and finally received a proper jacket, now on permanent display at the World Golf Hall of Fame in St. Augustine, Florida.

Each single-breasted blazer is embellished on the left handkerchief pocket with the Masters logo, made by AB Emblem Company. The buttons, also stamped with the same logo, are made by the Waterbury Button Company in Connecticut. Founded in 1812, the company boasts that "when Gen. Ulysses S. Grant met Gen. Robert E. Lee at Appomattox Courthouse, both men wore Waterbury buttons on their chests." Fashionable buttons for Brooks Brothers, J. Crew, and Rag and Bone are now part of the company's repertoire as well.

"Green jacket" knockoffs, ranging from $250 to $500, have been spotted on Internet auctions, yet a real Augusta National model is said to be truly priceless. Just ask four-time champion Arnold Palmer. He discloses that winning the Masters and putting on the green jacket is quite simply "one of the greatest things that can happen in a golfer's lifetime."

As the tournament comes to a close, the green jacket is carefully placed on a hanger, and the now-weary pilgrims will await yet another color-filled springtime in Augusta.

ABOVE: This button and others with images of the game can be found at flea markets and on the Internet and can be used to transform a sweater or jacket. **OPPOSITE:** For those who will never win or own a coveted green jacket from the Masters, there's a proper silk tie.

PAR-FECT PLATES FOR THE COURSE

Creating a golf-style table setting begins with color. A red place mat immediately conjures up the bold tartans of Scotland, while green evokes the fairways and putting surfaces on the course.

Pairing these colors with various china patterns of distinctive golf design or with motifs that allude to the game adds a sense of festivity to a post-tournament dinner, a ladies' luncheon, or an afternoon tea party.

Round green place mats echo the sphere of the golf ball when paired with Mikasa's Country Club china dinner plate encircled with golf clubs on a green border. A bread and butter plate displays a full image of a fairway, while the cup and saucer combine the two designs. A square silver napkin ring ensures that the circle theme is not overdone.

For a centerpiece, Steven Turner of Victoria Park Flowers Studio in Fort Lauderdale used a golf ball–type basket filled with balls and topped off with daisies. The hostess went to great lengths for the perfect place-card holders by having the bottoms of the balls cut off flat with a "slice" in the middle to hold the cards.

Fortnum & Mason's best tea suits a cup-and-saucer set by Royal Worcester called Hole in One. The red tartan creamer is made by Sasaki.

For an informal atmosphere, the hostess purchased faux grass accent pieces at Target and dropped a ball in the middle. A vivid red tartan dinner plate with gold rim from Royal Doulton is finished with a simple red-and-white check cotton napkin and a tortoiselike ring.

The best cut-crystal is brought out for a formal luncheon served on fine French china called Golf by Royale with small gold crisscrossed clubs. A salad plate in green and black tartan is made by Homer Laughlin, best known for their highly collectible vintage Fiesta ware.

THE

PART II

BACK NINE

REES'S MASTERPIECES

When golf course designer Rees Jones ponders the natural flow of the terrain destined to become one of his masterpieces, the land speaks to him. He walks the property and envisions the placement of tees, water hazards, and bunkers as he studies the topography.

"Primarily, the style of a course is dictated by the contours of the land," he says, adding that his goal is not to move all that much dirt. "Natural elements are embellished, and created components are finished to appear natural. Every design is customized to enhance what nature offers, always with sensitivity to environmental issues."

The impressive and demanding original designs done by Rees incorporate rocks, mounds, and bunkers of diverse depths and shapes, which resemble oversize puzzle pieces. The courses are situated along awe-inspiring ocean coastlines, on rolling meadows, in arid deserts, and even on a former Long Island potato field. They stretch from the London Hunt and

"The sharpest course designers put some wickedness into the holes."
—Lorne Rubenstein, A Season in Dornoch

Country Club in Ontario, Canada, to Blue Top Ridge at Riverside in Riverside, Iowa; the East Course of the Andalusia Country Club in La Quinta, California; and on to Kailua-Kona, Hawaii, at the Kohanaiki Golf and Ocean Club.

When asked to name a favorite course, Rees answers that it's difficult, adding, "The Ocean Forest Golf Club in Sea Island, Georgia, was a piece of ground with dunes, wetlands, and ocean. You just don't get all those natural characteristics at one time."

FAMILY VALUE

Rees's career path was a right of birth. Even those not intimately familiar with golf have heard the name of his late father, Robert Trent Jones, a prominent course designer. While growing up in Montclair, New Jersey, Rees tagged along to projects around the country, helping to measure tee locations and discuss hazard placements. He competed in junior golf as a young boy, and he played on the golf team at Yale while earning a bachelor of arts degree.

After graduate studies in landscape architecture at Harvard University, Rees immediately went to work for his father, running his East Coast office for ten years before opening his own business in his

hometown in 1974. In 1990, Rees purchased a 1907 shingle-style Victorian home zoned for commercial use in downtown Montclair. He executed a classic adaptation of the former home for reuse as his office building, skillfully illustrating that his design sensibilities are not limited to the outdoors.

Clients are greeted at the front door by an umbrella stand in the form of a golf bag. A small oval hand-painted ceramic medallion discreetly identifies the office address. The former living room has been transformed into an Oriental rug–lined reception area/work space. On the left, through vintage French doors, the old dining room now serves as a conference room with a custom-made conference table.

The geometry of the room dictated the length and width of the table, according to cabinetmaker Bob Weston, who designed and built it to fit the space using Carpathian elm burl and American black walnut.

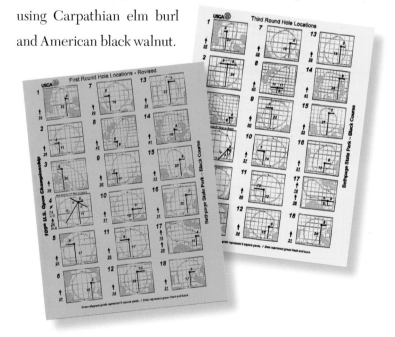

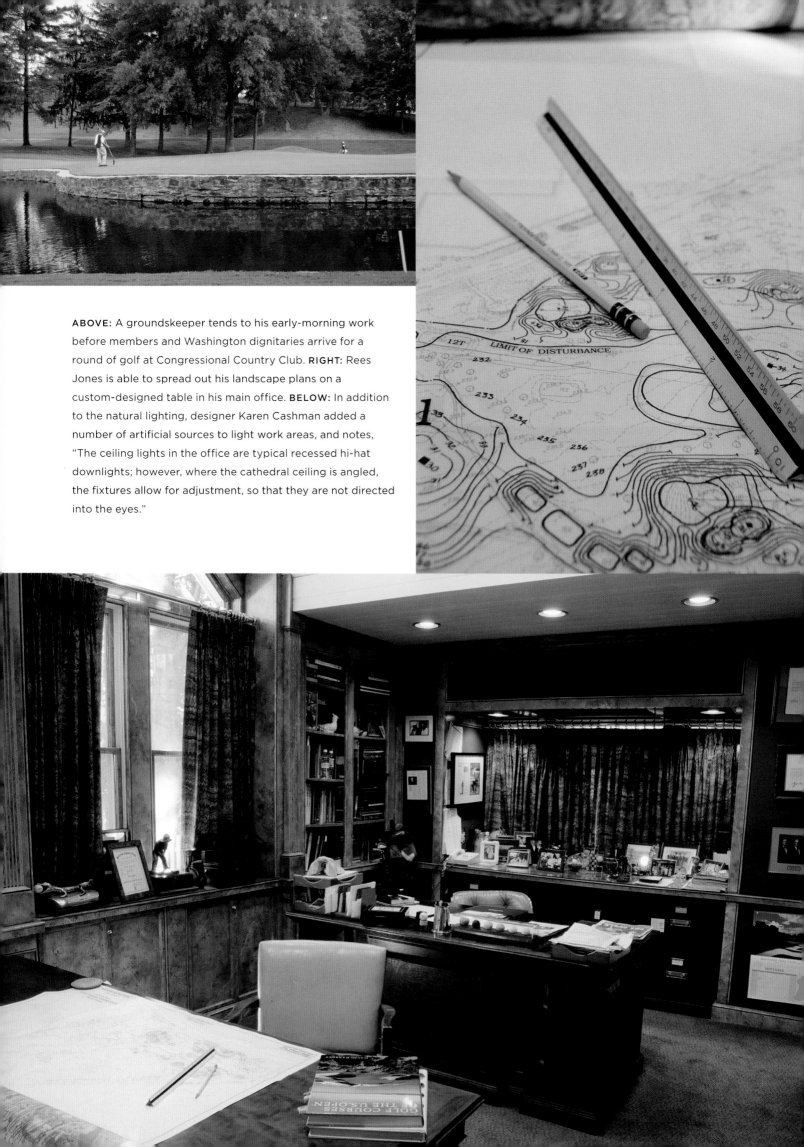

ABOVE: A groundskeeper tends to his early-morning work before members and Washington dignitaries arrive for a round of golf at Congressional Country Club. **RIGHT:** Rees Jones is able to spread out his landscape plans on a custom-designed table in his main office. **BELOW:** In addition to the natural lighting, designer Karen Cashman added a number of artificial sources to light work areas, and notes, "The ceiling lights in the office are typical recessed hi-hat downlights; however, where the cathedral ceiling is angled, the fixtures allow for adjustment, so that they are not directed into the eyes."

CLOCKWISE FROM TOP RIGHT: A photo behind Rees Jones's desk of the 1950 U.S. Open at Merion Golf Club with Ben Hogan, George Fazio, and Lloyd Mangrum holds special meaning as the first U.S. Open attended by a then eight-year-old Rees. Rees puts his signature on the course and on the ball. Formerly a dining room, the conference room offers a place to greet clients. "Rees's fine collection of commissioned paintings of his courses is hung throughout the building," says decorator Karen Cashman. An antique silver-plated inkstand. The expanse of the course commonly referred to as the fairway and rough is also known as "through the green." **CENTER:** Cabinetmaker Bob Weston designed a table of Carpathian elm burl and American black walnut to fit the conference room.

His artistic touches—the ebony wood inlay around the center burl field of the table, the detailed compass design on each corner—add depth. "The burl figure is actually the result of a cancerous growth on the trees, which creates the swirled and knot-filled pattern," he shares.

The legs are tapered pencil post with segmented molding at the top. The "lantern" at the top is made from poplar, overlaid with four pieces that match the burl. The intricate compass design in each corner of the tabletop is made in a sunburst pattern. Bob explains, "When the veneer is sliced at the mill, each piece is kept in order and saved in a group called a flitch in the same sequence that they are taken from the log. This gives me enough pieces to create the illusion of identical compasses in each corner."

Bob also finished the American black cherry desk in Rees's light-filled office in the rear of the house. Fashioned on the top and panels with tamo (Japanese ash) surrounded by movinqui cross banding with ebony inlay, it has an extraordinary touch. "As a little boy Rees played near his father's desk, which had secret compartments. He also wanted a desk with secret compartments, but I can't tell you where they are," Bob relates. Built-in cabinets hold papers and books, and a glass-topped expanse behind the desk, crowned with a display of family photos, partially conceals three file cabinets.

An oversize cherry worktable facing the desk, also made by Bob, provides space to spread out blueprints and maps. "We did not use exotic woods for this table since it was going to have papers on it all the time," he notes. Mementos around this room include an antique silver-plate golfer inkwell, an alligator eating a golf ball (an appropriate completion gift from the Dunes Golf and Beach Club in Myrtle Beach, South Carolina), and a collection of antique golf balls.

The plethora of awards Rees has won hangs on walls upholstered with a peacock blue wool broadcloth over Homasote (recycled papier-mâché wallboard). The treatment was chosen by interior designer Karen Cashman, who worked with Rees on the interiors. "Homasote was used so that blueprints could be pinned on the walls when need be," she recalls. "The office was drafty before reconstruction, and this also provided added insulation."

The custom moldings and woodwork were finished in a faux Parlino Cream green marble pattern. The Lee Jofa cotton sateen fabric for the draperies, in shades of green, terra-cotta, peacock, and umber, evokes fine old endpapers in a rare book. "Rees has an extensive book collection, which influenced the selection of the fabric design," Karen notes.

OPPOSITE: A clever umbrella stand is the only hint of golf in front of Rees Jones's purposely inconspicuous and unpretentious offices in downtown Montclair, New Jersey.
RIGHT: Bookends double as a decorative doorstop.

CAPITOL MAGIC

More than a hundred original golf course designs in thirty-five states and seven countries have come out of these offices. In addition, Rees is well known for his seventy-plus renovations; as an upshot, he has been nicknamed "the Open Doctor," a moniker also held by his father. Rees's work includes many of the game's most cherished courses—Pinehurst No. 2 in North Carolina, Long Island's Bethpage State Park Black, and the South Course at Torrey Pines in California—which must meet with standards set out by the United States Golf Association (USGA) in order to host a major championship. Much of the required renovation, such as lengthening the distance from tee to green, repositioning bunkers, and adding deeper layers of rough, are necessary because technological improvements in equipment result in the golf ball's flying farther than ever before. "The only reason to redo a course is to get a major championship," Rees states. "Courses for the average golfer do not get outdated."

At Congressional Country Club just outside the Washington, D.C., beltway in Bethesda, Maryland, Rees put his magic to work first for the 1995 U.S. Senior Open, a prelude to the 1997 U.S. Open, and then touched up the famous Blue Course once more for the 2011 U.S. Open. "It began with rebuilding the greens, and then the [USGA] committee began to look at a redesign. It's great they (the club) agreed to do it," he says, noting that the members of the club do not have use of the course during the many months of work. But they could play on the Gold at Congressional or at several nearby clubs offering temporary reciprocity.

Originally designed by Devereux Emmet and founded in 1921 by congressmen Oscar E. Bland and O. R. Lubring of Indiana, Congressional had an illustrious first president: Herbert Hoover, then secretary of commerce. Members have included Charlie Chaplin, Vincent Astor, Pierre S. duPont, William Randolph Hearst, and Walter P. Chrysler. Since then, presidents, congressmen, lobbyists, and diplomats have debated the merits of legislation while playing a friendly game of golf during the day, and danced to the toe-tapping society orchestra of Meyer Davis at weddings and galas in the palatial Mediterranean-style clubhouse at night.

Leading up to the 2011 U.S. Open, Rees visited Congressional, consulted with turf and irrigation specialists and construction and shaping crews, and occasionally spent the night in one of the club's guest rooms. In between traveling the globe for work, he carves out time to play fifty or sixty times a year as a nine handicap. His famous partners have included presidents Bill Clinton and George H. W. Bush and former New York City mayor Rudy Giuliani. Rees pronounces, "The best part of my work is the people and friends I meet along the way."

Dick Taylor, the late golf writer and founder of *Golf World* magazine, once referred to Rees Jones as "one of golf's treasures" and wrote, "You've got to believe this is a genius at work." As golfers of all levels step up to the tee and gaze down the exquisite and challenging fairways of one of Rees's many masterpieces, the terrain doesn't just speak . . . it sings.

BELOW: The AT&T National has also been held at Congressional. During the process of designing and renovating courses for major tournaments, Rees Jones consults with traffic flow experts and security personnel as well as turf specialists. During the event, at courses around the world, gaining access is all about having the right pass. Many seasoned spectators have learned that the ideal time to attend is during the practice rounds, when restrictions are not as stringent. **FOLLOWING PAGES:** A collection of rare antique golf balls adorns a side table in Rees's design studios.

FROM CALAMITY CORNER TO HOGAN'S ALLEY

In Noblesville, Indiana, golfers can test their skills at a club called Purgatory. "According to religious mythology, Purgatory is the place where souls pay for their earthly mistakes so they can gain entry to heaven," the website declares. "The name conjures images of struggling against great obstacles to achieve eternal happiness." Naming golf holes is an old-world custom, and in this case, the names of people and places in Purgatory have been used along with such deadly sins as "Pride."

From Pride, the golfer can proceed to "Stains of the Inferno," presumably another reference to Dante's literary classic, and on to the third hole, "Impenetrable Fortress." Some other notable holes around the world include:

Calamity Corner—No. 14 at Royal Portrush, Portrush, Ireland
Road Hole—No. 17 at the Old Course, St. Andrews, Scotland
Devil's Asshole—No. 10 at Pine Valley, Pine Valley, New Jersey
Island Green—No. 17 at Sawgrass, Ponte Vedra, Florida
Church Pews—Nos. 3, 4, and 15 at Oakmont Country Club, Oakmont, Pennsylvania
Valley of Sin—Eighteenth green at the Old Course, St. Andrews, Scotland
Himalayas—No. 6 at Royal St. Georges, Sandwich, England
Postage Stamp Hole—No. 8 at Royal Troon, Troon, Scotland
Amen Corner—Nos. 11, 12, and 13 at Augusta National, Augusta, Georgia
Bruce's Castle—No. 9 at Turnberry, Turnberry, Scotland

Feathery   Gutta-Percha   Hammered Gutta

"Although in 1893 it had been forty years since the introduction of the gutta-percha ball, many pros still affected 'the St. Andrews swing,' a closed choppy hack at the ball designed to draw and run the old featherie ball below the stiff Scottish winds." —Mark Frost, The Greatest Game Ever Played

Bramble   *Rubber Ball*   *Modern Ball*

FROM FEATHERS TO SLEAZE

A display in Rees Jones's office (previous spread) offers a brief visual history of the golf ball. On the far left, the vintage ball dating from 1830–1860, known as a "feathery," was made by stuffing boiled goose feathers (enough to fit in a top hat) into a piece of cow or horse hide, sewing it closed, and painting it white. When the feathers dried and expanded, the $1/2$-inch-diameter ball could reportedly fly as far as 250 yards.

The gutta-percha ball (known as a "gutty," second from left), made from the sap of the Malayan tree, first appeared in 1848 and was popularized by the mid-1870s. The aerodynamic patterns on the outer shell (third from left) of the painted white ball were first imprinted by hand.

The Haskell bramble, the first rubber-core golf ball (fourth from left), put into play in 1898, was said to add another twenty-five to thirty yards of distance. Notable variations followed, including the Worthington White in 1909, the 1914 Star Challenger, and the Faroid and the Burbank during the 1930s.

A red ball for winter play was popularized when writer Rudyard Kipling "invented" snow golf at his home in Vermont in 1893 and painted the balls bright red. Antiques dealer Dave Berkowitz of Golf's Golden Years has a rare Silver King red bramble circa 1915 and declares it's impossible to put a price on it.

For those who want to begin collecting, Dave suggests the Spalding Triangle with the triangle pattern, made in both the United States and the U.K. in 1920. For this ball in mint condi-tion, Dave Berkowitz estimates a price in the $200 to $300 range.

His massive inventory at www.golfsgolden-years.com has included the Map of the World golf ball (so named because of the image of a map embossed on the surface) made by J. P. Cochrane & Co. of Edinburgh around 1912. Dave notes, "This has always been one of the most desirable unusually designed golf balls ever made. With no cuts or nicks and virtually all of its original paint, a ball such as this would easily sell for upwards of twenty-five thousand dollars."

And a word of advice: "No logo balls like those from universities, breweries, clubs, and tournaments," Dave cautions—even major tour-naments. "These will always be three-dollar balls."

Tom Rhodes, a retired engineer, carves clowns, pirates, and other caricatures out of old golf balls. Gary Shienfield took the after-market idea to new heights when he started GolfBallsOnly, one of the world's leading recy-clers of "certified pre-owned and refinished name brands."

And finally, collectors looking for wit over value might consider www.sleazeballs.net, a business that grew after its first edition with Ber-nard Madoff's image on the aiming sweet spot. Offerings include O. J. Simpson, Osama bin Laden, and Kim Jong Il, along with political types from both sides of the aisle. "Optimum spin for maximum duplicity, tournament-quality golf balls with 432 dimple design, two-faced preten-sion, and sham cover," the website states.

11

Byrdies

Amanda and Jonathan Byrd's low-country beach cottage on St. Simons Island, Georgia, exudes Southern charm. With a courting swing and a rocking chair on a spacious front veranda, it's a splendid spot for the couple to take in the soft Atlantic Ocean

breezes while spending time with their young children, Caroline and Jackson. The exterior tabby finish of oyster shells mixed into stucco and the handmade wrought-iron railings contribute to the convivial character of their home. Dating to the 1600s, the tabby overlay technique was once considered of humble Spanish and Moorish origins. The lime and sand–based texture is now a coveted element.

For Jonathan, who travels the globe as a world-class professional golfer, living on the twenty-seven-mile-long, three-mile-wide island offers a chance to practice at the Sea Island Golf Club between tournaments. Returning to the tranquillity of an exquisite home after dizzying rounds of golf also means precious time with his family and friends.

PREVIOUS PAGE: Byrds on a swing: Jackson, Jonathan, Amanda, and Caroline.
CLOCKWISE FROM TOP LEFT: Jackson Byrd practices his swing in the backyard. The early beach cottages on St. Simons were built on logs and rolled away from the ocean every twenty years or so in order to avoid erosion. "It was a logic and simplicity of ages past," says contractor Steven Schoettle. The Byrds' home is a contemporary interpretation of that style with the same exterior tabby finish of oyster shells mixed into stucco. Jonathan and Jackson share a few father-son moments following a "practice" round of golf in the backyard. Golf style comes in the form of a fancy bib for Caroline. St. Simons Island has 234 holes of golf, three clubs, numerous resorts, and charming accommodations for vacationing duffers.

COASTING ALONG

The small-town atmosphere of the island becomes obvious on weekends, when enthusiastic residents telephone one another: "Turn on the television; Jonathan's playing." This low-key lifestyle also affords Jonathan the opportunity to carpool for nursery school and playdates, or to spend a simple afternoon in the backyard showing the next generation the subtleties of the game. "During a week off I look forward to coming home and relaxing," he says. "Eating dinner with my family at home and playing with my kids in the backyard is the best way to unwind after a busy few weeks on tour."

Amanda worked with interior designer Beverly Olliff and contactor Steven Schoettle to carry out the renovation she and her husband envisioned. "Beverly gave us great choices when it came to fabrics and furniture that fit into our color scheme and budget," Amanda recalls. "We chose what we liked the most and she pulled it all together. She kept the feel of the home casual, Southern, and coastal with a great mix of antiques and pieces that are durable enough to withstand lots of family playtime."

"We gutted half the house," Steven explains. "The majority of the work was in the existing shell of the home." Tearing out dated Spanish floor tiles and installing oak floors throughout created a uniform appearance and flow.

In typical Southern fashion, the Byrds' home includes a formal dining room just off the center hall. The walls are finished in a light blue with ivory trim. "There are no hot colors here," discloses Beverly, who has owned Southern Interiors, now in St. Simons, for almost four decades. A round mahogany dining table from the British company Bevan Funnell presides, with chairs upholstered in a textured ivory silk. The silk draperies from F. Schumacher are in an ivory and

ABOVE: Since turning pro in 2000, Jonathan Byrd has enjoyed life on the twenty-seven-mile-long, three-mile-wide island that takes on a small-town atmosphere as neighbors call one another on Sundays when he's playing on the tour. **BELOW:** The first lighthouse erected on the south side of the island was destroyed during Civil War skirmishes in 1862 and a second lighthouse was built in 1872. It is now operated by the Coastal Georgia Historical Society.

aqua plaid, the predominant colors throughout the home. Decorative artist Josie Kennedy was called in to faux finish the drapery rods, finials, and brackets. "I used a cream color with blue and gold and then a raw umber glaze over it."

"The nice thing is the Byrds and Beverly had definite ideas, which made it easier to determine how we would use certain colors," Steven says. The decisions on how to incorporate architectural elements were also easy. Two large columns flanking the entrance to the dining room were removed: "They created a visual block, and it didn't fit the area. It wasn't in keeping with the architecture of the house. Some people think more complex forms make a home fancy," Steven asserts. "This only makes it trendy." The dainty chandelier from Currey & Co. of Atlanta "gives a delicate feeling to the room," Beverly adds.

A ROOM OF HIS OWN

Jonathan's office is masculine with touches of golf style. Custom-made French Creole doors in Spanish cedar wood, which echo the vernacular style of the front door, open into the space. "The proportion defines it as Creole," says Steven, who designed a hand-forged wrought-iron bracket for Jonathan to hang a collection of pin flags in his office.

Also on display are mementos of his 2002 Buick Challenge, 2004 B.C. Open, and 2007 John Deere Classic victories, as well as numerous reminders of his days spent playing for the Clemson University golf team.

"It's his room," Beverly notes. "Everything is relative to his career and his family. They're just warm people, and it shows with all the photographs around the room. He's a celebrity who is just a nice guy." So nice is he, in fact, that when a starstruck delivery man arrived during the renovations, Jonathan gave him a tour and sent him off with an autographed photo.

OPPOSITE: In true Southern form, the Byrds have a formal dining room. The round table is made of mahogany, and the six chairs are covered in an ivory silk. The formal flavor continues with a small living room with a fireplace, French-inspired antiques, a crystal lamp, and a large upholstered table several shades darker than the dining room chairs.

ABOVE: Golf mementos from his days playing on the Clemson team as well as traveling on the professional tour are now part of Jonathan's home office.

BIRDS ON DISPLAY

A tour for all visitors includes the comfortable great room, a place for family time with an informal dining area, a television, and a fireplace. Horizontal whitewashed one-by-twelve boards define the room as wainscoting, and a sisal rug reinforces the coastal informality. "A lot of what we did was to integrate things to make sense," Steve says. "It's comfortable, and even before the furniture was moved into place, there was warmth, and then it became a home." Flanked by blue and sea-foam-green swags, transom windows with three-quarter-height shutters above offer a flood of natural light.

The great room gives way to an open area in a formal living room with a fireplace, French-style antiques, a crystal lamp, and a large upholstered table in a soft taupe. Just across the hall is the renovated kitchen. The original one was demolished, and the essential triangular flow from work area, stove, and sink was rearranged, with an island installed that features a hidden warming drawer. The bricks behind the cooking space extend to the floor for an old-world feel, and the cabinets were finished with a tea glaze to accentuate the moldings. Throughout the house, reminders of the family name appear in such forms as a bird atop the paper towel holder or a decorative touch on the back of a chair.

Wherever possible, cabinets, doors, and electrical outlets have been childproofed with safety latches, doorknob covers, and outlet covers throughout the house. Each child has a room to suit—shell pink for Caroline and soft lime green for Jackson. Closets were remodeled to keep clothing racks at the children's eye level, and Dutch doors suggest independence to the young occupants, while a nearby parent can still keep an eye and ear on things.

For Dad, staying in shape by cross training is a vital part of his career on the PGA Tour, so a space above the garage was converted to a personal gym. Skylights lend natural light, and wall-to-wall rubber floor mats were installed, along with a television. A music system imparts inspiration while Jonathan jogs on the treadmill or lifts weights.

"We love every room in our house," Amanda pronounces. "It's delightful to come home and settle in after being on the road."

OPPOSITE: According to decorator Beverly Olliff, everything in Jonathan's room relates to his career. This includes flags from notable tournaments, artwork, badges, and medals. **CLOCKWISE FROM TOP LEFT:** The family emblem can be seen everywhere. Son Jackson's room is painted a soft lime, and little Caroline's room is painted shell pink. Three-quarter-height shutters with transom windows above offer a flood of natural light in a more relaxed area of the great room where friends and family gather.

12

ONE MOMENT IN TIME

Arriving in the golf mecca of Pinehurst, North Carolina, often produces a dizzy sensation as one drives around the circular streets searching for the Pinehurst Resort, the Holly Inn, the Magnolia, or the Tufts Archives.

Then, suddenly, it's all about Olmsted.

Frederick Law Olmsted Sr. (1822–1903) is best known as the prolific landscape designer responsible for New York City's Central Park, the Biltmore Estate in Asheville, North Carolina, and hundreds of other parks and college campuses. He did not believe in right angles or the grid-pattern street layout.

In 1895, the firm of Olmsted, Olmsted & Eliot was retained to design the previously unnamed village in the Carolina Sandhills for a fee of $300. Their philosophy of sweeping, scenic circular thoroughfares and public open space was ultimately executed

by colleague Warren Manning after Frederick Law Olmsted exhibited early symptoms of senility.

The Olmsted firm had been hired by New England pharmacy store entrepreneur James Tufts, who purchased 5,890 acres for just over $1 per acre. He also acquired the naming rights for what officially became the Village of Pinehurst after he read a list of names that had been rejected for development on Martha's Vineyard. Thirty cottages and numerous rooming houses were constructed in crisp white frames with accents in Pantone color 343, forest green, on shutters and awnings. All were named after popular New England plants, such as Oak, Hanover, Mistletoe, and Cedars, as well as the Holly Inn, which anchors the center of town. Brick sidewalks and punched-brick serpentine walls are signature touches. The massive four-story, 250-room Carolina Hotel sprang up, as well as a firehouse, a butcher shop, and markets for locally grown flowers, produce, and dairy products.

Golfers took over the fields near the dairy farm, and James Tufts requisitioned the first six-hole course, constructed in the cow pasture. Leonard Tufts, his son, inherited the venture when his father passed away in 1902 and immediately expanded the original golf course. In 1900, he hired the legendary designer Donald Ross and built three more courses. Golf and Pinehurst had now become one and the same.

TUFTS STUFF

Richard Tufts, who captained the winning 1963 U.S. Walker Cup team, took over leadership of Pinehurst from his father, Leonard, in 1928. In 1970, Richard brokered a $9 million sale of the resort to a large corporation, and in 1975, he created the Tufts Archives, a treasure trove of family photos, records, and memorabilia, Donald Ross's golf course plans, and the original Olmsted maps.

Located in the back of the Given Memorial Library, a one-story Colonial Revival with Flemish bond brickwork and tetra-style portico on the original village green, the Tufts collection includes one of James Tufts's marble-and-silver nineteenth-century Arctic Soda Fountain machines, old hickory sticks, and eighty thousand photos illustrating local history.

A portrait of Richard Tufts painted by Beth Turner flanked by a pair of vivid red leather wingback chairs and a display of old trophies decorate a reading nook dedicated to the Tin Whistles. Formed in 1904, this group of men would arrive at the tenth hole of Pinehurst No. 1 and blow a whistle. It was the signal for liquid refreshment, perhaps a wee bit of scotch brought out to the "thirsty" players as they made the turn to the back nine. The Tin Whistles are still in existence today, along with their female counterparts, the Silver Foils, founded in 1909.

PAGE 161: Located behind the Pinehurst Country Club, the Putter Boy statue seen here in a circa-1960 photo was sculpted by an unknown artist. PREVIOUS PAGES: Clare Booth Luce, Alexander Haig, Elizabeth Dole, Phil Donahue, and Elton John have all experienced the Southern charm seen in the lobby of the graceful Pinehurst Resort. OPPOSITE, CLOCKWISE FROM TOP LEFT: The Tufts Archives at the Given Memorial Library offers a treasure trove for researchers. A small painting of Donald Ross and an old wooden tee marker. Antique clubs, old china from the resort, books, and photos fill the main room at the Tufts Archives. A puzzle from the 2006 U.S. Open at Pinehurst. A peek into a trophy display case at the Pinehurst Resort. The Olmstead architectural firm's plans for the Village of Pinehurst.

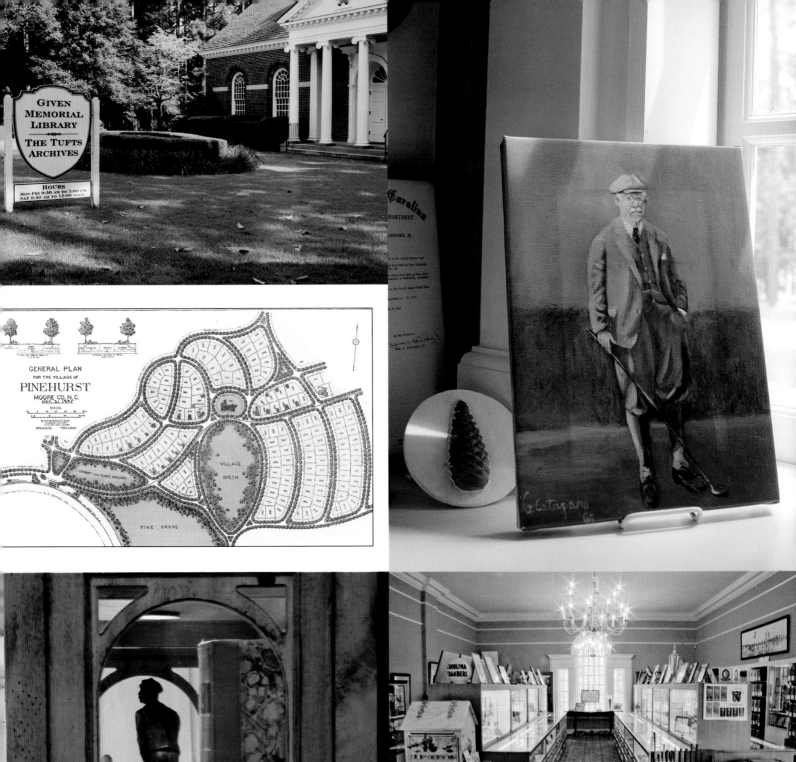

OPPOSITE: In the reading room at the Tufts Archives, the portrait of Pinehurst founder Richard S. Tufts was painted by Beth Turner. THIS PAGE: Vintage golfing trophies in a pine secretary at the Pinehurst Resort add to the ambience.

OPPOSITE, CLOCKWISE FROM TOP LEFT: The Reverend Billy Graham, one of a steady stream of well-known personalities who have found time for a round of golf in Pinehurst, once said, "The only time my prayers are never answered is on the golf course." All of the original lodging facilities in Pinehurst were named after popular New England plants such as Oak, Hanover, Mistletoe, and Cedars, as well as The Holly Inn. While stationed at nearby Camp McCall during the 1940s, bandleader Glenn Miller often entertained and played golf at Pinehurst. Here he discussed a different type of swing with Dick Haymes, an Argentine actor and famed vocalist. During his tenure as vice president, Richard Nixon took time out to greet other guests visiting Pinehurst. Ben Hogan spells out victory following his 1942 win in the North-South Open. A visitor makes a close putt. Actor Don Ameche visited the home of Pinehurst friends Mr. and Mrs. O. V. Russell on Midland Road. The pine trees remain an iconic image in Pinehurst; only the prices have changed. **THIS PAGE, CLOCKWISE FROM TOP LEFT:** During the 1940s, men's golf fashion in North Carolina included plus fours and spectator-type shoes. Caddies were offered reduced fare on the trains from New York City to travel south for work during the winter in Pinehurst. General George C. Marshall, who maintained a home in Pinehurst, takes a stroll with 1952 Amateur champion Barbara Romack. A young golfer begins to perfect his swing in this 1939 photo. The clean white signs with Pantone number 343 forest green accents still dominate the thoroughfares in the village. **CENTER:** Arnold Palmer with Pinehurst-based photographer John Hemmer.

LEFT: A banner from the 1999 U.S. Open hangs above a tall glass-top custom-made vitrine that holds old bag tags, caddy passes, and other mementos. **ABOVE:** The bar area of the golf-themed game room at Rivas House accommodates several dozen guests. **BELOW:** As one of thirteen original cottages along Midland Road that back up to the famed Pinehurst No. 2 course, the circa-1938 Rivas House has undergone several significant additions to the left of the central entryway and to the right with an oversize wing that includes the game room and additional garage space.

RIVAS HOUSE

In 1999, Karen and Tom Linton found their way to the Village of Pinehurst from the Midwest and bought their wood-frame and stone Colonial Revival home. One of thirteen original cottages along the No. 2 course, their "Rivas House" was built in 1938 by Helen Woodward Rivas, daughter of Orator Frank Woodward, who owned the patent for Jell-O.

"This house was not originally a home to live in," Karen explains. "It was a getaway place. The only reason to be here is for golf, but I didn't want the entire house in golf."

Beginning with a well-traveled pool table, which has been in previous Linton homes in St. Louis, Chicago, and Grand Rapids, the transformation of the home included adding an outsize game room dedicated to golf. There is an old British feel to the room, with the warm rich wood pool table as the centerpiece and dark green walls and plaid wall-to-wall carpet that suggest a Scottish ambiance. A long open bar adds to the relaxed atmosphere. Display shelves built beneath the staircase contain son Ryan's trophies from the golf team at the University of Southern California. A painting by Richard Chorley of the fifth hole at No. 2 holds a special place along one wall. The distinguished British artist is celebrated for his detailed depictions of prominent golf courses around the world.

"It puts the home and the room in a historical perspective," says local antiques dealer Tom Stewart, who represents the artist. "The house is on the fifth hole of No. 2, and this painting shows the same view as is seen from the backyard. The Lintons did a fastidious job, and it only makes sense to use such an authentic piece in the room."

MEMORABLE MOMENT

The 1999 U.S. Open will forever be remembered by all who attended and watched the final moments of the tournament in Pinehurst.

As the sun sets and players wrap up yet another battle with their scorecards, a long walk on the pine needle–covered sand-based fairways leads up to the final hole of the famed Pinehurst No. 2. On this last green, Payne Stewart sank a memorable fifteen-foot putt for par to win the 1999 U.S. Open.

Three months after that magnificent victory, the forty-two-year-old golfer was a member of the winning U.S. Ryder Cup team at The Country Club in Brookline, Massachusetts. Six weeks later, he died in a bizarre airplane accident when a suspected oxygen leak triggered depressurization in the cabin, killing all six occupants. Television viewers around the world followed the tortured path of the chartered Learjet 35 as it flew eerily on autopilot in what was scheduled as a routine trip from Orlando to Dallas. When the fuel supply was exhausted, the plane crashed in a South Dakota field. Payne Stewart and Pinehurst became linked forever. His victorious gesture after sinking that final putt to win the Open—pumping his right fist into the air and kicking up his right leg—has been immortalized in a dramatic, larger-than-life bronze by sculptor Zenos Frudakis.

Overlooking the very same eighteenth hole at Pinehurst No. 2, it is called *One Moment in Time.*

FOLLOWING PAGES: The golf-inspired décor in the game room of the sprawling Rivas House includes British artist Richard Chorley's detailed landscape of Pinehurst No. 2, as viewed from the backyard of the home. A collection of family trophies, framed posters, and other memorabilia have been incorporated as accent pieces.

Official Stroke Card
99th United States Open Championship®
Questions as to the Rules of Golf shall be referred to the USGA Rules Committee

For USGA Use
Previous Total _____
This Round __68__
New Total _____
Verified: 18th ___ Pr. ___ Pub. ___

Competitor STEWART, PAYNE

Round 1 Date 06/17/99

HOLES	1	2	3	4	5	6	7	8	9	OUT	10	11	12	13	14	15	16	17	18	IN	TOTAL
YARDS	404	447	335	566	482	222	398	485	179	3,518	610	453	447	383	436	202	489	191	446	3,657	7,175
PAR	4	4	4	5	4	3	4	4	3	35	5	4	4	4	4	3	4	3	4	35	70
	4	4	3	5	4	3	4	4	3	34	4	4	4	4	4	2	4	3	5	34	68

Marker's Signature _Jeff Maggert_

Competitor's Signature _Payne Stewart_

GREAT GOLF SITES TO VISIT

United States Golf Association Museum and Library, Far Hills, New Jersey

American Golf Hall of Fame, Foxburg Country Club, Foxburg, Pennsylvania

Ralph W. Miller Golf Library and Museum, City of Industry, California

World Golf Foundation, World Golf Village, St. Augustine, Florida

British Golf Museum, Bruce Embankment, St. Andrews, Fife, Scotland

North Berwick Museum, School Road, North Berwick, East Lothian, Scotland

The Heritage of Golf Museum, Gullane Golf Club, Gullane, East Lothian, Scotland

Royal and Ancient Golf Club, St. Andrews, Fife, Scotland (by invitation only)

Royal Troon Golf Club, Troon, Ayrshire, Scotland

Japan Golf Association Museum, Shijimicho Miki-shi, Hyogo-ken, Japan

Valderrama Golf Museum, San Roque, Andalusia, Spain

TOP LEFT: After playing a round, Pinehurst visitors will discover all types of golf-related gifts, jewels, and antiques at venues such as this one. **TOP RIGHT:** Payne Stewart's first round score card from the 1999 U.S. Open in Pinehurst. **ABOVE:** Sculptor Zenos Frudakis's bronze of the late Payne Stewart, *One Moment in Time,* is located by the eighteenth green of Pinehurst No. 2, not far from where Stewart won the 1999 U.S. Open. **OPPOSITE:** The fifth hole of Pinehurst No. 2.

13

SOPHIE'S CHOICES

The foundation of women's golf fashion has remained traditional and timeless, with an emphasis on ease of movement while playing. The imagery of the game is also an element of daytime attire off the course—golfer silhouettes on scarves or needlepoint clubs and balls on belts and shoes.

Tasteful innovation while on the course began in 1904 with Thomas Burberry's debut of the Free-stroke Coat, which had ample sleeves designed to allow the ladies' arms to move without restraint. Burberry, a former draper's apprentice, opened his London shop in 1856. He also invented and patented gabardine, a water-resistant wool, in 1888.

During this era, female golf costumes usually comprised a long skirt and a plain blouse. This utilitarian ensemble may have made a proper fashion statement, but the fitted blouse encumbered the dynamics of swinging, and the club often became

Sophie Gustafson
at Magnolia Grove
Robert Trent Jones Golf Trail

Mitchell
Tournament of Champions
presented by
Kathy Ireland Worldwide
LPGA November 2005

© Frank DiVita 2009

entangled in the skirt. So Burberry, already noted for sporting garb, popularized a golfing skirt that could be raised up eight inches during play by using a drawstring. Around this same time, the distinctive black, white, and red "Burberry check" first appeared as a trench coat lining. Now a registered trademark, it's frequently spotted on golf courses around the world in the form of umbrellas, scarves, and jackets.

The female golfing dress of choice during the early 1900s continued to be a blouse and a skirt with a jacket. Starting around 1909, women began wearing cardigan sweaters instead of the jacket, and around the same time, argyle first appeared. Derived from the tartan of Clan Campbell in Argyll, Scotland, the two-color diamond pattern is placed diagonally in a checkerboard or overlapping arrangement, which appears to portray a sense of three-dimensional texture and movement. Argyle continues to be a staple in golf fashion on hats, gloves, visors, socks, and belts. In the same era, the straw boater with a bow became the hat of choice of champion Harriot Curtis (1881–1974).

By 1920, golfing skirts were just below the knee, and they continued to be popular until a one-piece dress that became known as a shirtwaist hit the racks. Introduced in 1929 by Best & Co. of New York and widely imitated, it remained a bestseller for golfing and nongolfing women for several decades.

De De Johnson, a Los Angeles–based designer in the 1950s, created a below-the-knee golf short that resembled a pleated high-waisted skirt with a matching belt. The long shorts allowed female golfers even more flexibility and comfort as they played the game. By the late 1950s, it also was becoming acceptable for women to wear knee-length Bermuda shorts on most courses.

As more women began to take up golf during the 1960s, the ladies sports apparel company Leon Levin came out with the "Q" skirt, or "skort," a combination of shorts and skirt, which remains a trendy choice to this day.

PRIMARY CHOICES

The below-the-knee shorts preferred by Swedish-born professional golfer Sophie Gustafson were once known as pedal pushers. Sophie, who started playing golf at age ten and turned pro in 1992, has had a number of victories on the LPGA circuit and in other international competitions. Tall and statuesque, she has a swing that artist Frank DuVal, who follows the LPGA circuit, has studied and describes as "clean and athletic. She rotates her upper body considerably, with power and grace," he states.

Sophie has played for the European team in seven Solheim Cup events, the preeminent match

PAGE 177: Artist Frank DuVal's pen-and-ink and pencil sketches such as this one of Sophie Gustafson and of other competitors on the LPGA tour have tapped into a previously ignored portion of the art market, which has typically focused on the men's events and sweeping vistas of the fairways. OPPOSITE: The sweeping lines of women's golf attire have always been the definition of decorous.

CLOCKWISE FROM TOP LEFT: Women golfers circa 1930. As seen in this antique print from the 1800s, golf has always been a family outing. In the early 1930s, women golfers' skirts began to get shorter than the full-length versions of previous years. A heavy rainfall during the Trans-Mississippi Golf Tournament, June 7, 1937, in San Antonio, Texas, failed to dampen the spirits of the lady golf stars, some of whom are shown here: Opal Hill, Bea Barrett, Marion Miley, Patty Berg, Betty Botterill, and Lucille Mann. A photograph from 1937 depicts streamlined attire accented with the popular spectator-type golf shoes. OPPOSITE, CLOCKWISE FROM TOP LEFT: Mrs. Donald Parson (left) and a friend circa 1915 illustrate the long skirts that were still in vogue. The young caddy accompanying these women around 1895 was often asked to help tee up the ball before the ladies stepped up to play. Wearing a belt over a sweater, which also happens to be popular today, provides more room for making big swings. Originally manufactured by Max Factor with an Art Deco style of artwork intended to appeal to golfers, the Outdoor Girl line included face powder and rouge. The painted tin containers are now considered collectibles. Women golfers in Pinehurst circa 1930. Mildred "Babe" Zaharias, winner of the 1954 U.S. Women's Open at Salem Country Club in Peabody, Massachusetts, autographs the cast of Joe Dey, executive director of the United States Golf Association.

CLOCKWISE FROM TOP LEFT: The two-tone diamond pattern of argyle has remained a design element in golf fashion since it first appeared around 1909. The shoe on Sophie Gustafson's shelf was autographed by her fellow European team members playing for the Solheim Cup, the preeminent match play international tournament in women's golf. Sophie Gustafson, who frequently wears clothing from Cutter & Buck, became the first woman to compete in a men's event at the Casio World Open in Kaimon, Japan, in 2003. The styles range from skirts to skorts and shorts at practice time during Golfari, a five-day ladies-only semi-annual clinic held at Pine Needles. In a professional career spanning twenty-five years on the LPGA tour, Rosie Jones almost always favored a minimalist look of Bermuda shorts, a polo shirt, and a visor. Upon her retirement at the U.S. Open in 2006, Rosie took off her shoes and gloves and left them by the eighteenth hole at the Newport Country Club.

play international tournament in women's golf. One of Sophie's sponsorship agreements provides a wardrobe of Cutter & Buck golfing outfits to don during tournaments around the world. This includes an open-sleeve polo shirt tailored by Cutter & Buck so as to not inhibit Sophie's magnificent swing.

Fashion and function haven't always gone as hand in hand in women's golf. Today professional and amateur female players prefer to wear their shirts out, and if they want to make a real fashion statement, many wear a belt over top since it is less likely to inhibit movement that way.

At the towering height of six feet, up-and-coming professional Michelle Wie dons the Nike line of clothing in everything from a very short skort in warm weather to long pants and a Therma-FIT zip jacket for the cold climate in Great Britain. Seven-time LPGA winner Paula Creamer is known as the Pink Panther for her favorite head-to-toe fashion statement, which even extends to the bright pink balls she uses.

PRIMARY COLORS

In addition to ease of play, color has also become a factor when women make golf fashion choices, and Irene Filacchione has found a niche therein. "Colors brighten the spirit," she notes. Where else to begin with vibrant colors but on the golf course? "Live a little," Irene says. "I had this idea, and that's it. I was looking for colors that provoke a reaction." Her Connoisseur Collection of shirts, vests, fleece jackets, and quilted jackets in bright purple, sea-foam green, turquoise, royal blue, and vivid green with khaki accent pieces can be layered. Fabricated to "feel like cotton," Irene's "own concoction of artificial fibers moves with you when you swing, doesn't stick to you, and will dry quickly."

ABOVE: For the PGA Tour Wives Association charity event at the Honda Classic, the fashions include shorts, skorts, and skirts in a sea of pastels at the PGA Resort and Spa in Palm Beach Gardens. Fifty percent of the funds raised go toward the Nicklaus Children's Health Care Foundation, and the rest is given to other charities along the tour. **BELOW:** Needlepoint designs inspired by the game for this pair of fashionable mules offer a chance for ladies to step out in style while off the course.

Golf has not only provided inspiration for clothing worn by women while playing; it now extends to other fashion-related accessories that stylish ladies wear off the green, such as Susan Inman and Judith Tytrel's silk scarves. They combined their fondness for golf with a bit of entrepreneurship when they started their business, Barth and McCallig, in 2007. After meeting at the U.S. Open at the exclusive Winged Foot golf club in Mamaroneck, New York, where their husbands are members and frequent playing partners, Susan and Judi recognized a need.

"There were no scarves to buy," says Judi, an attorney in New York, who volunteered as a marshal at the 2006 Open at her home course. Susan, an airline attendant, was helping in the merchandise tent and noticed that men shopping during the tournament struggled with sizes when they tried to purchase a gift for their wife or a lady friend. "A great scarf fits anybody," Judi adds.

Wanting to create a high-quality scarf such as those from Hermès or Gucci, they chose to create a silk one with hand-rolled edges, gorgeous colors, and an attractive presentation. "The color is important," says Judi. "The designs are one thing, but when there's color, that's everything." Employing six colors, they launched seven designs with imaginative names

OPPOSITE: Women's fashions today include these colorful silk scarves, which can go from the course to the clubhouse with very little effort. Knotted loosely at the waist, they double as a belt. Inspired by history as well as the game itself, Susan Inman and Judi Tytrel's line of scarves includes patterns such as "The Dames" (opposite, above right; and this page, below right) and "It's in the Bag" (opposite, below). **THIS PAGE, LEFT:** Inman and Tytrel's "The Language of Golf." "Its circular design moves us from the rough to the fairway and from the bunker to the green with maybe a mulligan or two," Susan notes. **ABOVE RIGHT:** A colorful scarf is part of a layered look when paired with a sea-foam-green vest and jacket designed by Irene Filacchione, which moves with ease from the putting green to the patio for an après golf celebration.

including "The Language of Golf," "It's in the Bag!," and "The Dames."

WAIST MANAGEMENT

Using similarly imaginative names for her designs—"Hole in One," "Pink Golf Bag," and "Golf Course Views"—Barbara Story launched her needlepoint venture. She got her inspiration for the business from her husband. "He was always wearing needlepoint belts," she explains. Now her Philadelphia-based company, Itz a Stitch, provides custom-embroidered belts, mules, and shoes that are hand-stitched in Europe and sold in shops around the country.

The ancient craft of needlepoint is created on an open-weave canvas with yarn. Evidence of a similar technique has been found in Egyptian tombs, on ancient Maori costumes in New Zealand, and on medieval religious vestments. Barbara's vibrant patterns of golf balls, tees, clubs, and even putting sequences replicate symbols of the game.

While traveling to Romania to visit relatives, she learned they had been sewing belts, so she struck a deal. "They said if I paid them they would make belts for me, so I started emailing designs to them." A team of designers, many from Philadelphia College of Textiles and Science, execute her colorful visions on the mesh canvas before they are stitched. Some of the pieces include custom designs. "We actually made a birthday belt for Arnold Palmer in seven days," she says, as opposed to the normal three- to four-week process.

Traveling to sales and marketing events, Barbara does find time for a bit of golf. "I have a thirteen handicap," she reveals.

HUNG UP

If Sophie were searching for the ultimate hanger to use for her golf wear, she might turn to Jeff Keller's clever design. Fashioned from a golf club, the perfectly balanced piece serves as a functional addition to the closet or as a gleaming example of three-dimensional wall art.

The Logan, Utah–based artist declares that design is his passion. He began salvaging bicycle rims and repurposed them as hangers, which sold very well. Yearning to create a hanger representing another sport, Jeff opted for golf. He spent many sleepless nights sketching a prototype and poring over notes on how to make sure the golf club would fit on a rod.

"I wanted the lines to be simple with clean angles," Jeff recalls. "That's what golf is, elegant and simple. It transforms the smooth chrome and the grip and the balance. What a surprise. This is functional art."

OPPOSITE, CLOCKWISE FROM TOP LEFT: In order to play golf and still remain fashionable, many women have opted to wear their belts over their shirts, allowing ease of movement while swinging and putting. For her line of golf-inspired needlepoint belts, Barbara Story used recurring imagery of the game in miniature: the shoes, the clubhouse, and of course the ball. Alternatively, a favorite scarf can look smart as a belt, as spotted on this spectator. **ABOVE:** Designer Jeff Keller spent long hours perfecting his golf club hanger, which can also serve as a sculptural decorative element.

LADY'S LIDS

Vicky Waldorf, the wife of pro golfer Duffy Waldorf, and her longtime friend Cindy Gilmore found time for golf style in the form of their basic yet oh-so-elegant Gogie Girl caps. The idea arose from the two women constantly wearing their husbands' hats as they ran errands during their busy days in Southern California. Says Vicky, "They were simply guy's baseball-style caps. I did have one hat that was sent to me by the UCLA Alumni Association that was fairly comfortable, and I decided to embellish it with a few Swarovski crystals. I showed my good friend Cindy (a fellow mom with four children at the same school that our children attend) the embellished hat and Cindy thought it was cute." Vicky continues, "After a few months of homework, we realized that there wasn't really any headwear company out there focusing solely on women's baseball-style caps."

Gogie Girl made its first sale in June 2007, and the caps are now sold around the world. The company also often donates to events that raise awareness for breast cancer, ovarian cancer, and heart disease. "We were able to donate six hundred hats to a nonprofit organization to deliver to women and girls in Kenya. They have very little, and we are pleased to help provide some cover from the daily hot sun on their faces. Our motto is and has been since day one Gogie Cares."

Gogie Girl's distinctively feminine and stylish caps have lively and expressive accents such as polka dots or twinkling Swarovski crystal embellishments, which Vicky and Cindy personally apply. Clearly, ladies on the links these days have come a long way from high-buttoned shirts, long skirts, and the straw boater worn by Harriot Curtis in 1910.

ABOVE and BELOW: Vicky Waldorf is a hands-on designer with her own line of Gogie Girl caps, which are sold around the world. She spends every spare moment affixing Swarovski crystals onto them in various designs. **OPPOSITE:** The neon pastels of Lilly Pulitzer have been a popular fashion statement on the golf course for many decades.

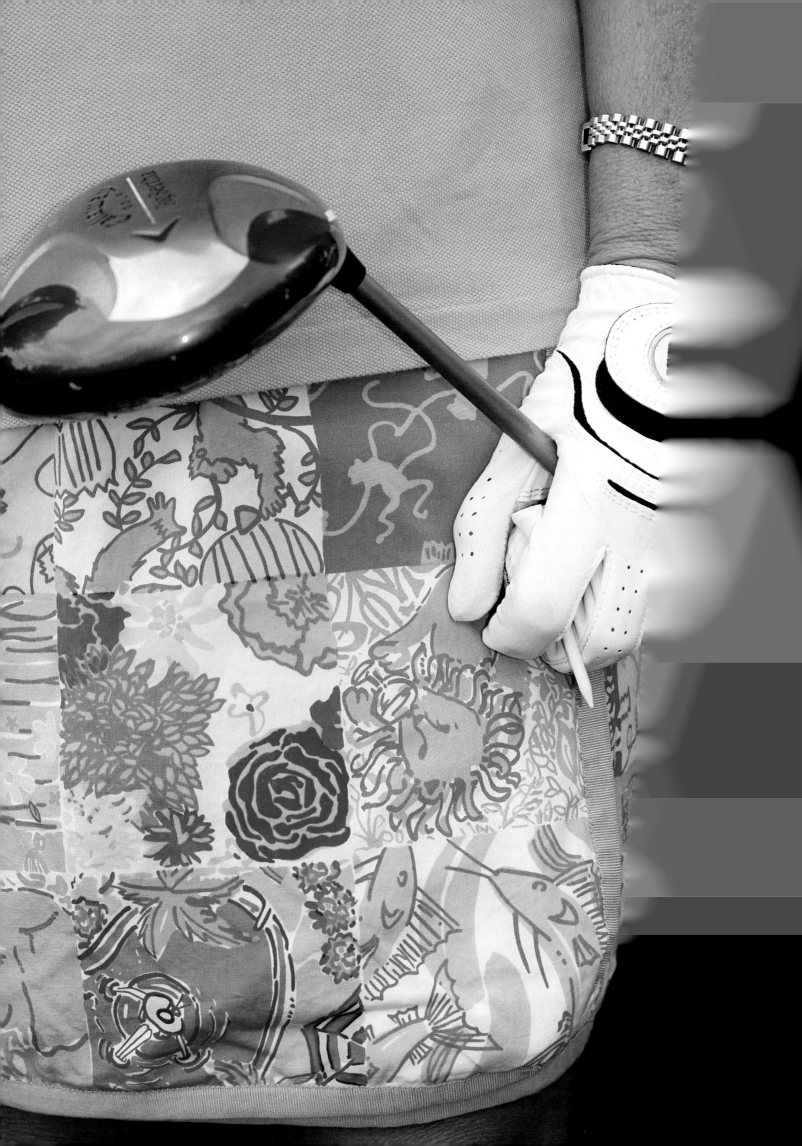

14

DUFFY'S VINTAGE VANTAGE

When Vicky and Duffy Waldorf moved to their Mediterranean villa in Northridge, California, their first priority was to have room to stretch out. With four growing children—Tyler, Shea, Kelli, and Justin—involved in diverse activities and hosting a spate of visiting friends, the time had come to move.

For Duffy, a colorful contender on the PGA Tour since 1985, there's also the wine. The easygoing California native is known for his fine ball striking, a looping swing, colorful shirts, and an intense interest in wine.

As a young man emerging from UCLA with the California State Amateur title and college Player of the Year honors, Duffy was introduced to wine appreciation by his father. "We started on white Zinfandel," he recalls, adding that his early palate went

from light beer to such notable collegiate vintages as Cold Duck, Ripple, Mateus, and Lancers.

His tastes advanced to Chardonnay and then Merlot as he struck out on the professional golf circuit. "Every bottle was different, but not necessarily good." When he married fellow Californian Vicky in July 1988, their newlywed apartment in Chatsworth included a fifty-bottle oak box on the floor. "It looked like a college fridge," Duffy recalls.

As Duffy's golf travels expanded, his wine collection followed. The Waldorfs' next home, in Sageus, had a seven-foot-high double-door cellar, and eventually, he recalls, "the idea of collecting just came into being. My first years as a pro I'd come home with a new bottle of wine from Asia or Australia. Wow, you get to try their version of wine. Then to Italy and the varietals that you may not have had, like Sangiovese or Trebbiano."

While traveling on the PGA Tour these days, Duffy often purchases six bottles or an entire case at a time. "We enjoy it over the years, and some of the bottles won't be touched for ten years," he says. Following decades of travel, tasting, and reading, Duffy's expertise led to his own wine column, "Uncorked," for *Golf* magazine. "Smoke and chaparral on the nose, fresh and full-bodied on the release, smooth and silky as it goes down. Still offers plenty of flavor after fifteen years," he writes of a 1993 S. Anderson Richard Chambers Cabernet Sauvignon.

For their most recent cellar, the couple spent a full year on the renovations. "I could see that the feng shui was totally wrong," Duffy reveals. "So we totally scrapped everything and started over." The Waldorfs designed their ultimate glass-enclosed wine cellar adjacent to the dining room. "He had his eye on this space when we looked at the house," Vicky says.

With an eighteen-hundred-bottle capacity, the cellar holds nostalgic bottles of Thunderbird and Ripple and vintages such as a 1976 bottle of Château Lafite Rothschild. There's also an ample supply of the owner's signature line of wines: Duffy Waldorf Syrah, Chardonnay, Zinfandel, Cabernet Sauvignon, Sauvignon Blanc, and Pinot Noir.

The Waldorfs entertain frequently, often inviting friends for a tasting of a Shiraz or a special bottle of Bordeaux. Such an event involves planning and timing, Duffy notes. "It can take three days for a good red wine to open up once I've uncorked it," Duffy explains, "and then the peak drinking window can be hours or days."

For a dinner party, Duffy believes the wine should dictate the food, as opposed to the usual method of asking a local wine merchant what to serve with chicken or fish. "Find the bottle you want to offer your guests and then work from there," he suggests with a smile. "By pairing the wine with the right foods, you start to learn the meaning of marriage, and I'm not just talking about my wife."

PAGE 191: "I keep my cellar at fifty-three degrees [Fahrenheit]," says professional golfer and wine aficionado Duffy Waldorf. "The difference between fifty-three and fifty-five degrees can be significant over a twenty-year period since the wine evolves more slowly." OPPOSITE: Duffy Waldorf's victories on the PGA Tour include the 1995 Valero Texas Open, the Buick Classic and Westin Texas Open in 1999, and the 2000 National Car Rental Golf Classic Disney. His collection includes many trophies as well as this commemorative gift from Augusta.

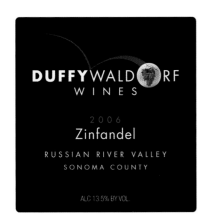

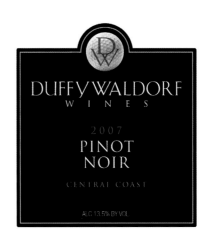

NICKNAMES

As a young boy tagging along with his grandparents on the golf course, James Joseph Waldorf Jr. earned the nickname "Little Duffer," which evolved to Duffy. Other notable golf nicknames include:

The Merry Mex—Lee Trevino
The Golden Bear—Jack Nicklaus
The Shark—Greg Norman
Boo—Thomas Weekely
Veej—Vijay Singh
Lefty—Phil Mickelson
Zinger—Paul Azinger
The Big Easy—Ernie Els
Boss of the Moss—Loren Roberts
DL3—Davis Love III
The Mechanic—Miguel Ángel Jiménez
The Duck—Angel Cabrera
Ollie—José María Olazábal
Wee Icemon—Ben Hogan
Babe—Mildred Zaharias
Wiesey—Michelle Wie
Boom Boom—Fred Couples
El Niño—Sergio Garcia
Gentle Ben—Ben Crenshaw
The King—Arnold Palmer
Slammin' Sam—Sam Snead
The Squire—Gene Sarazen
Wild Thing—John Daly
The Pink Panther—Paula Creamer

OPPOSITE, CLOCKWISE FROM TOP LEFT: The Waldorfs' collection of glass and crystal awards includes stemware that comes in handy for entertaining. "Most wine has flavor; it's the structure and balance of the tannins, acid, and fruit that give character," Duffy Waldorf notes as he and wife, Vicky, prepare for guests. Twenty-five percent of their eighteen-hundred-bottle collection is from California; the rest comes from around the world. **ABOVE:** As a young boy tagging along with his grandparents on the golf course, James Joseph Waldorf Jr. earned the nickname "Little Duffer," which eventually evolved to Duffy. He went on to succeed on the PGA tour before developing his own line of wine.

TEE TO TEA

Duffy Waldorf is not the only professional golfer in the wine business. Australian native Greg Norman, winner of the 1993 British Open and seventy other tournaments, produces California and Australian wines. Annika Sorenstam has set records on the women's tour in ninety victories. In 2009, Annika Syrah was introduced by Wente Vineyards in California. Seattle native Fred Couples, a fifteen-time PGA Tour winner, including the 1992 Masters, collaborated with Napa-based winemaker Mitch Cosentino to create two Cabernet Sauvignon blends.

From South Africa, ten-time PGA Tour winner David Frost followed his family into the wine business. Fellow South African Ernie Els, a three-time Major champion with more than forty wins worldwide, teamed up with Jean Engelbrecht of Rust en Vrede to create a five-varietal Bordeaux called Ernie Els Stellenbosch.

When not doing commentary for CBS and the Golf Channel or working on golf course design, Great Britain's Nick Faldo also dabbles in wine. The Nick Faldo Selection Cabernet, Shiraz, and Sauvignon Blanc are offered through Katnook Estate of South Australia.

Canadian Mike Weir decided to showcase the wines of his home country at his winery near the Niagara Parks Whirlpool Golf Course. His Chardonnay and Cabernet Merlot are produced by Château des Charmes in Niagara-on-the-Lake.

At the breathtaking Trump National Golf Club in Rancho Palos Verdes, which hugs the Pacific coast, golf and wine can be combined in a tee time followed by Wine 101, a series of classes offered by the in-house sommelier.

The ice buckets, wine racks, sleek glass-top tables, and wire or wooden chairs used at Trump National are golf-inspired items from designer Steve Shatkin. The legs of the various pieces resemble the head of a wood driver, and Steve says he tried to be as golf-authentic as possible. "The grips used on the back of the chairs and bar stools are real grips custom laser-etched with our logo, and the wood feet used on the tables and shelf displays are custom turned from real persimmon wood, just like the drivers in the old days."

Also in Napa there is the wine of the legendary Arnold Palmer, known in golf circles as "the King." In 1996, he partnered with Luna Vineyards beginning with Pinot Grigio and Sangiovese and then extending to Arnold Palmer Cabernet Sauvignon and Chardonnay. The daily Golf Wire e-mail hailed his Cabernet Sauvignon as having "amazing intensity on the entry, with a tannic, broad structure."

Finally, for teetotaling golfers, there's the thirst quencher originally concocted when Arnold made a request to a bartender at the Cherry Hills Country Club in Denver. The idyllic mix of iced tea and lemonade is known simply as an "Arnold Palmer," a refreshing nonalcoholic libation that is definitely fit for a king.

15

SWING BLING

Golf bling comes in the form of sparkling trophies, dazzling jewelry and accessories, even a twinkling tee made of gold or silver.

The style is always elegant. Wearing too much flashy jewelry while playing on the golf course can cause a distraction, and baubles can become intertwined in clothing. Any type of garish display would also be considered in poor taste according to the hushed mantra of the sport. According to one golf devotee, the flicker of a diamond tennis bracelet signals just that . . . "for tennis." Instead, golf style might call for a single well-worn gold bangle in the sleek form of a golf club encircling a lady's wrist, or a glistening trophy that serves not only as a reminder of victory, but also as a clever way to add a hint of glint to home decor.

Treasured golf objects not won in a fair and square competition can also be purchased. Found at flea markets, antique shops, and even on the Internet, the challenge of discovering a glimmering trophy is almost equal to the thrill of victory strolling up to the clubhouse.

SPARKLING TROPHIES

Antique trophies reveal the rich history of the game. Golf-mad enthusiasts sometimes incorporate their collection into the home or office as objets d'art, accent pieces, even as vessels for fruit or flowers. A tall old silver trophy can be repurposed as a lamp with some wiring. A small silver piece found at an antique market makes a memorable gift to celebrate a special occasion such as graduation or a birthday. The original engraving adds to the allure, and the gift will maintain its value or perhaps appreciate in value. Displayed on a bookshelf or on a desk, the piece also holds a sentimental value.

One of the finest examples of old trophies is on display at the United States Golf Association museum in Far Hills, New Jersey—a colossal eighteen-karat piece of golf bling that the U.S. Amateur Champion receives for his winning swing. Dating to 1895, the towering sixteenth-century-style Havemeyer Trophy steeple cup is named in honor of the United States Golf Association's first president. The original trophy, a silver cup, was destroyed in a fire, and this version, created in 1926, was presented by USGA treasurer Edward S. Moore.

By far the most stunning trophy for women is the Robert Cox Cup, which goes to the winner of the U.S. Women's Amateur Championship. The statuesque silver cup also holds the distinction of being the only United States Golf Association trophy donated by someone outside of the United States. When Cox, a graduate of the University of St. Andrews, a Scottish member of British Parliament, and a golf course designer, floated his generous offer to the USGA, they first did an extensive background check on the Edinburgh native. Cox had one condition in return. After falling in love with Covent Station, New Jersey, he stipulated that the championship be held at Morris County Golf Club.

The two-foot-high Etruscan-style sterling silver trophy is the oldest surviving trophy for a USGA championship. Produced by silversmith George W. Shiebler & Co. of New York, it was first awarded to Beatrix Hoyt in 1896. Vibrant Scottish-inspired enamel overlay in a green-and-purple plaid wraps around the base with the seal of St. Andrews. Leaves of emerald-and-violet thistle weave around the bottom, leading to a piece of art showing St. Andrews Castle on one side and a view of the golf course on the other. Topaz cairngorms surround the top and the cover, where a beautiful Scottish thistle tops off another enamel panel with a woman golfer and a scene from St. Andrews.

New York City–based Tiffany & Co., founded in 1837, produced the one-of-a-kind custom-designed PGA Tour Northern Trust Open trophy, Arnold

PAGE 199: The ultimate gift of bling for any golfer is a sterling-silver tee from Tiffany. OPPOSITE: The trophies of Zimbabwe native and professional golfer Denis Watson include the 2007 Senior Open championship, second from left, beneath the portrait of his winning putt at the event in Kiawah Island, South Carolina. The bronze statue for the 2008 Ben Hogan award is given by the Golf Writers Association of America.

OPPOSITE: Artist Tom Pinch's portrait of the late beloved Payne Stewart clutching the U.S. Open trophy following his 1999 victory. **ABOVE:** This well-used and cherished family silver water pitcher was won by Harold F. Banister at the Thousand Island's Country Club in 1927. "We use it at all big holidays, birthdays, and anniversaries," says Betsy Banister, whose late father-in-law was the golfer in the family. At all other times it doubles as a vase for flowers, ferns, or eucalyptus.

CLOCKWISE FROM TOP LEFT: Danny Lee with the eighteen-karat U.S. Amateur championship trophy that he won in August 2008. Designed by Tiffany, this sparkling trophy is for the winner of the Bay Hill Invitational at Bay Hill, Florida. A portrait of Ben Hogan by J. Anthony Wills is on display at the USGA Museum in Far Hills, New Jersey, along with replicas of the Claret Jug, presented to the winner of the British Open; the U.S. Open trophy; and the Ben Hogan commemorative box from the Masters. A replica of the U.S. Women's Amateur championship trophy, the Cox Cup, is presented to Amanda Blumenherst at the scenic par-three seventh hole, following her August 2008 victory in the final round of match play at Eugene Country Club in Eugene, Oregon. Given in 1896 by Robert Cox of Edinburgh, Scotland, the Cox Cup is the only USGA trophy donated by a person from another country. Champion Ben Hogan received this gold medal and wicker-basket flagstick following his victory at Merion Golf Club in Ardmore, Pennsylvania. The unusual baskets have been in place at the exclusive club since course designer Hugh Wilson introduced them in 1912.

Palmer Invitational trophy, and PGA Tour FedExCup trophy. They sell all types of golfing bling, from a key chain in the form of a club to a sterling silver tee to be used for decorative purposes only—on a desktop or a shelf—since the tee frequently goes astray when one hits the ball. (Some of the wooden tees break in pieces, and others are never to be found.)

Tiffany was also responsible for the sterling silver creation commissioned by businessman John Watson Cox of New York City sometime between 1902 and 1907 and awarded at the Oakland Golf Club, one of the most affluent clubs in the city. Estimated to be worth more than $100,000, it's now part of the Greensboro, North Carolina, museum of Replacements, Ltd. The trophy was intended to honor Irish immigrant John B. McDonald (1844–1911), a self-taught engineer responsible for the New York City subway tunnels and a prominent member of Oakland Golf Club. The intricately embellished trophy is adorned with oak leaves at the top and bottom, an image of McDonald, and the engraving THE OAKLAND GOLF CLUB MCDONALD TROPHY. Along with the logo on the bottom, the letter *C* denotes Charles T. Cook, president of Tiffany president at the time the trophy was made.

ABOVE: Known simply as the Claret Jug, the trophy for the British Open championship was first awarded in 1873 and now resides permanently at the Royal and Ancient Golf Club in St. Andrews. **LEFT and BELOW:** The Oakland Golf Club McDonald Trophy was to honor Irish immigrant John B. McDonald (1844–1911), who belonged to the Oakland Golf Club. Silver experts are able to identify the era on a vintage piece of Tiffany silver by the stamped marks on the bottom. A letter (the *C* here) identifies the last name of the company president at the time the item was created.

DAZZLING JEWELS

Other companies that made golf silver include Gorham, Wm. B. Kerr & Co., and Frank M. Whiting and Co.; their hallmarks can usually be found on the bottom of the item. Many of the pieces made from 1890 to 1940 came from Unger Bros., a Newark, New Jersey–based manufacturer noted for pocketknives. Designed by Emma Dickinson, whose husband, Eugene Unger, owned the company, the Art Nouveau golf-associated match safes, coin purses, and desk accessories can be found at antique shows and shops around the country and are not only highly collectible but also quite valuable.

Following in Emma Dickinson's footsteps, Catherine Canino is today's golf jeweler of note. The New York City–based designer draws on the classic, impeccable lines of the club or the arch of the ball in bracelets and necklaces. She issues three collections per year, based on the fashion and colors of the seasons.

A graduate of the Rhode Island School of Design, Catherine began her creative career designing jewelry for Ralph Lauren before setting out on her own. Adorned with pearls and semiprecious stones and heavily augmented with sterling silver, pieces include a bracelet with a toggle clasp in the shape of a tee or a golf ball-embellished bangle.

"I realize that women are passionate about their sports and love to flaunt their passion, jewelry being an excellent way to do so," Catherine says. Feeling that the golf jewelry market was encumbered by either clunky cheap pieces or diminutive expensive ones, she uses the iconic images of the game in a fresh way. "The largest consumer of this line is women making self-purchases, which is very satisfying to me."

Gemologist and goldsmith Patricia Reil sells her pieces to women, as well as to men on a golf outing in the Village of Pinehurst who want to bring a trinket home to their wives, girlfriends, or daughters. Juxtaposing "links" and "golf" in an all-new way, Patricia spends two or three days creating each piece in a space set up in the back of her shop, Jewels of Pinehurst. Among her most popular articles is a fourteen-karat-gold golf ball bracelet.

LEFT, TOP TO BOTTOM: Found at antique and specialty shows, this sterling match safe dates to 1890. This circa-1900 coin purse is silver-plated, and this circa-1900–1910 sterling-and-enamel match safe is highly sought after. **ABOVE RIGHT:** Between one and two inches in diameter, these sterling-silver pillboxes are circa 1900–1920.

CLOCKWISE FROM TOP LEFT: Catherine Canino's bracelets are made of sterling silver with her signature toggle closure, which incorporates a golf tee. This reproduction pillbox of faux diamonds and malachite may not be a real antique like those in the display case in which it was found, but it is the perfect keepsake, birthday gift, or holiday surprise. A quick eye at a flea market spotted this silver golf bag ladies' lapel pin. In her Pinehurst-based studio, goldsmith Patricia Reil puts the finishing touches on a golf ball bracelet. Details on one of Canino's twisted silver cuffs include the club head.

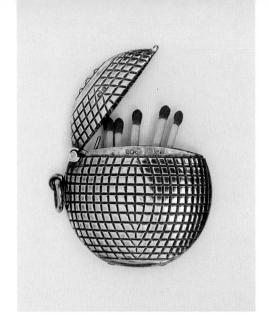

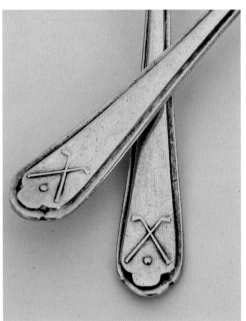

TWINKLING TEES

The definitive piece of golf style bling also comes in gold, this one in the form of a tee. Nancy Mailliard, president and owner of the Northern California–based Mailliard Designs, came up with the idea to create a gold tee after taking up golf a decade ago. "I've been hooked ever since," she notes.

"During my travels and visits to some of the most beautiful courses in the world, I saw a need for a high-end gift that could be personalized with a course logo, or someone's initials," recalls Nancy. "Thus, a memento to treasure."

Placed on a stack of books or papers on a desk, the shimmering tee is a gentle reminder of happy days out on the fairways. Many mementos are simply to be treasured. Hitting a ball off a solid gold or sterling silver tee will not improve your score, and wearing gleaming gems will not lower your handicap . . . but it will certainly add some bling to your swing.

CLOCKWISE FROM TOP LEFT: Made by H.W. Ltd. in Birmingham, England, this circa-1905 sterling silver match safe in the form of a golf ball measures 1¾ inches in diameter. Contemporary bling can be purchased at golf tournaments around the world in the form of commemorative money clips. These silver-plated teaspoons circa 1940–1950 were probably once part of a country club collection. **OPPOSITE:** For an elegant statement in adaptive reuse, a silver candlestick has been wired and mounted as a lamp and topped with a golf-style shade, and a silver champagne bucket trophy has a second purpose for masses of white hydrangeas.

16

TREASURES AND TOMES

For those who are passionate about the sport, collecting golf treasures, from ceramics to clubs to books, has now become a spirited sport unto itself.

A few rare birds collect golf-related antiques but don't even play. For many others, collecting golf memorabilia arose from a hobby of collecting antiques of all kinds, which became more focused after they took up the game. Such was the case with Tom Stewart, who started collecting forty-some years ago. As a young boy employed as a caddy by day and watering fairways and greens by night in his native Michigan, he admired the old photographs displayed at the country clubs where he worked. As an adult, he began what became his own extensive collection.

PREVIOUS PAGE: Tom Stewart regales customers at his Pinehurst shop with great golfing lore. A must-stop for visitors to the region, the store offers everything from paintings to collectible scorecards, trophies, lamps, and books. **ABOVE:** Made by Dartmouth Pottery, Ltd., this large pale blue mug was manufactured in the late 1940s. **OPPOSITE, ABOVE and BELOW:** The form on this colorful contemporary platter echoes the silhouetted golfer on the early-1900s porcelain bisque plaque.

Following a career as a touring and teaching professional, Tom launched his golf antique and book business in Pinehurst, North Carolina, in 1997. The Old Sport & Gallery is located in the Harvard Building, once a circa 1897 hotel. Now, with every sale of a painting, a book, or an old photo, Tom regales visitors with grand old tales of his youth, when, as an ambitious ten-year-old, he walked miles to get to a club where he caddied for $1 a bag. As one of the first members of the Golf Collectors' Society, Tom suggests that to add a touch of golf style to the home and office, one or two key accent pieces can set the tone. A small grouping of golf-associated beer steins, mugs, vases, or bowls can be the foundation for a larger collection.

According to collectors and dealers Sally and Wayne Perkins of Evansville, Indiana, also members of the Golf Collectors' Society, worthy pieces to consider include the hand-painted porcelain made by the Ceramic Art Company; Dickensware pottery from Weller in Zanesville, Ohio; Doulton stoneware made in England at Lambeth; Kingsware earthenware made by Royal Doulton; and Royal Doulton's Gibson Series Ware.

"The best way to learn about ceramics is to go to antique shows—not just golf antique shows, but any large antique show," Wayne advises. "You'll always find dealers who are willing to share information and advice."

One of the most popular lines among golf collectors is the Royal Doulton Golf Series Ware, featuring images by the British illustrator Charles Crombie (1885–1967) that first appeared in a 1905 book, *Rules of Golf*, published by Perrier Water in France. Eight golfers and caddies were shown on earthenware pieces, hand-colored and glazed in shades of ivory and yellow, marked with the Royal Doulton imprint, and noted as pattern numbers 3395, 3394, and 5960. Pieces in this collection can be found in the form of candlesticks, plates, sugar casters, and loving cups adorned with one of five amusing rules of the game:

1. *He that always complains is never pitied.*
2. *He hath good judgment who relieth no' wholly on his own.*
3. *Give losers leave to speak and winners to laugh.*
4. *All fools are not knaves, but all knaves are fools.*
5. *Every dog has his day and every man his hour.*

THIS PAGE, LEFT TO RIGHT, TOP TO BOTTOM: The finds of Evansville, Indiana, collectors and dealers Sally and Wayne Perkins include: a plate from the Arnold Palmer line of china, a contemporary pitcher with the image of *The Blackheath Golfer* by Lemuel Francis Abbot, a porcelain match bowl by Wiltshaw & Robinson, a vase from Weller Dickens Ware circa 1900s, a three-handled loving cup with a silver rim by Ceramic Art Company, a Weller Dickens Ware vase, a Kenlock Ware creamer in black, a stoneware pitcher by Doulton Lambeth circa 1900, a green Wedgwood-style slipware pitcher, a Rockwood Pottery cigarette holder circa 1950, a contemporary blue golf-motif mug from Spode, and silver-rimmed stoneware by Doulton Lambeth.
OPPOSITE: a stoneware pitcher by W. T. Copeland & Sons, a terra-cotta-colored Kenlock Ware creamer produced by Wedgwood from 1900 to 1931, a Crown Staffordshire porcelain teacup and saucer circa 1930, the reserve side of a contemporary pitcher, a character jug by Royal Doulton circa 1970, a Weller Dickens Ware vase, an earthenware pitcher by Royal Doulton Kingsware, two Golf Series Ware two-handled cups by Royal Doulton, Golf Series Ware by Royal Doulton, Golf Series Ware teacup and saucer by Royal Doulton, a teapot of the same vintage, a hand-painted early 1990s beer stein by Ceramic Art Company for O'Hara Dial Company, a Weller Dickens Ware vase, and a small Gibson Series Ware vase by Royal Doulton made from 1904 to 1918.

GOLF de la Soukra TUNIS

FÉDÉRATION DES SYNDICATS D'INITIATIVE DE TUNISIE

IMPRIMERIE DE VAUGIRARD, PARIS — AOÛT 1932

ROGER BRODERS

TO A PUTTER

Little Putter, smooth and shining,

Short of stature you may be,

But there's room for no repining

That you cannot sweep the tee.

For the driver, tall and slender,

And its brother brassey, too,

Neither, in their pride, can render

Greater services than you.

Boastful of their ball-compelling

Power, they may show you slight.

But the part you play is telling:

Potent is your touch so light.

Moments multiplied make ages;

Little drops, the rolling sea;

Little putts, say golfing sages,

Make the sum of victory.

So, my modest little putter,

Teach your lesson day by day.

Trifles, more than tongue can utter,

Make or mar both life and play.

—Francis Bowler Keene, 1899

MORAY FIRTH COAST

GREAT NORTH OF SCOTLAND RAILWAY

GOLF COURSES at LOSSIEMOUTH · SPEY BAY · BUCKIE · CULLEN · PORTSOY · BANFF · MACDUFF · ROSEHEARTY · FRASERBURGH · CRUDEN BAY

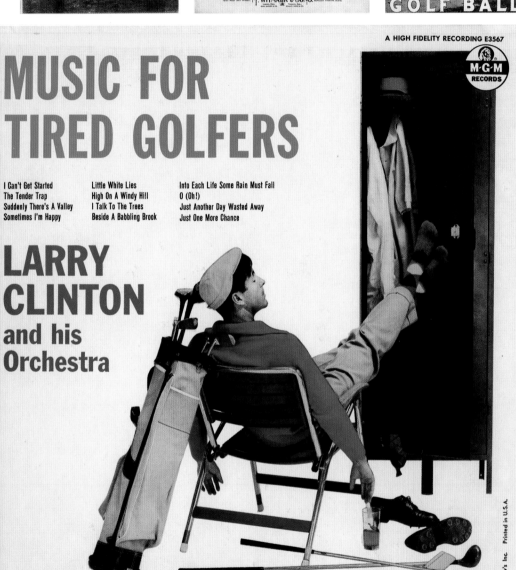

OPPOSITE: Golf-related travel posters, one from France, circa 1932, *Golf de la Soukra Tunis,* and another from the Moray Firth Coast, Great North of Scotland Railway, for stops at golf courses at Lossiemouth, Spey Bay, Buckie, Cullen, Portsoy, Banff, Macduff, Rosehearty, Fraserburgh, and Cruden. **CLOCKWISE FROM TOP LEFT:** Charles Sands at the tee during the 1900 Olympics at the Compiègne Golf Course in Paris. Sheet music such as that for "The Golf Club" is a rare find. A circa-1923 golf-ball poster from Spalding. A vintage Rex golf-ball poster. Old golf-ball boxes are collectibles. Old 33⅓-rpm records and covers can be discovered at garage sales and at auction.

EASTERN BENGAL RAILWAY

SHILLONG
THE GLENEAGLES OF
INDIA

THE CADDY

MARCH AND TWO STEP

BY

Fred T. Ashton.

Published by JOS. W. STERN & CO. 34 & 36 W. 28th St. N.Y.

CLUBS

Old wooden golf clubs are collectible as decorative pieces and as valuable antiques. Prized for their elegant, spare beauty, they are displayed as artwork in their own right, and have also sometimes been repurposed as artwork on a larger scale.

Florida sculptor Norm Gitzen created a magnificent piece of art with used golf clubs under the coffered ceiling in the bar area at the Wanderers Golf Club in Wellington, Florida. Norm teamed with interior designer Marcel Maison, who had created a

similar piece with polo mallets at the International Polo Club Palm Beach. The client now wanted to recreate the concept using golf clubs.

"I started out counting how many clubs I was using and lost track," says Norm, who specializes in creating large-scale pieces out of his cavernous studio not far from the golf club. One of the three hundred clubs used in the intricate sculpture once belonged to daredevil Evel Knievel.

If it would take a keen eye to spot a celebrity collectible such as Evel Knievel's red, white, and blue club, it would take a bona fide expert to unearth a long-nose putter stamped "A.D.," attributed to Andrew Dickson, credited as the first ever caddy during the 1680s. He later became a club maker. This rare club, offered in the record-setting Sotheby's auction of the Jeffery B. Ellis Collection in New York City, is a fine example of a valuable antique. Sold as lot number 260 in September 2007, the sensuous ash club pulled in $181,000 from an anonymous bidder. But novice golf collectors need not despair: decorative clubs can be found at flea markets and garage sales, on eBay, and in antiques shops for as little as $10 each.

Discerning duffers who want to begin collecting antique clubs as individual pieces or in sets sometimes consult with Bob Pringle in Troon, Scotland. "A set of golf clubs from the period of 1770 to 1830 would comprise a play club or a driver, three spoons of varying lengths, a putter, and either one or two iron clubs," says Bob, owner of Old Troon Sporting Antiques.

PAGE 218: Framed and matted, vintage-style posters like this one are an uncomplicated approach to adding a touch of golf style to a room or a hall. PAGE 219: Vintage golf-inspired sheet music is a creative decorative piece when framed as well as a highly sought-after collectible due to the sheer scarcity of the subject matter. ABOVE: A clever way to display antique clubs is to build a custom case to be mounted on the wall. Here the green felt back accents the wood. OPPOSITE: To fill the void in the coffered ceiling of the bar area at the Wanderers Club in Wellington, Florida, sculptor Norm Gitzen created a sculpture using old golf clubs.

CLOCKWISE FROM TOP LEFT: A quiet corner in a Fort Lauderdale sunroom, surrounded by reminders of a memorable trip to the golf mecca of St. Andrews, Scotland, draws extra illumination from a small golfing lamp, offering the ideal place for the lost art of writing a thank-you note or even a book on golf style. A portrait of Francis Ouimet by Rusty Jones is the backdrop for a vignette at the USGA Museum showing a set of irons Ouimet used in his 1913 U.S. Open win. A miniature porcelain golf bag opens to reveal a tiny tee and ball. Collectors will discover many items in what is known as the merchandise tent during the Open in Great Britain. A cozy golf-style niche can be achieved by adding a tartan throw, lamps with a golf motif, and strategically placed accent pieces.

Bob's inventory in the past three decades has included a rare and unusual center-shafted driver with torpedo-shaped head and brass sole plate by "Simplex," circa 1897, and a long-nose aluminum-headed spoon, the BS2 model by the Standard Golf Company of Sunderland, circa 1905. Some of these clubs resemble a garden tool or a potential murder weapon more than an implement for the intended purpose, and prices range from $100 to $40,000.

The clubs, with wooden shafts made of exquisite hickory, hazel, ash, lancewood, lemonwood, and greenheart, are works of art. Many are made by storied club makers like William Park, Robert Forgan, Hugh Philp, and James McEwan.

For those who want to add a handmade replica to their collection, Australian Ross Baker is the go-to club expert. Ross got hooked on the game after tagging along as a caddy with his father and then working in a pro shop. "It was at fifteen that I started tinkering with clubs and mending them," he remembers.

A year later he left school and began training as a golf professional, which requires comprehension of the club making, teaching, and shopkeeping elements of the trade. Ross notes, "I spent a lot of time making new clubs, repairing broken clubs, and experimenting with woods and irons."

As his interest in the history of golf grew, Ross began to study the golf clubs early players used and then started replicating them. "After doing a lot of research into the types of timbers, the tools used, and the methods of construction, I started to make long-nose clubs myself," he says.

Since 2004, Ross has demonstrated his craft each year at the Australian Open, crafting a long-nose wooden putter completely from scratch, cutting out and rasping the wooden head to shape, planing the

ABOVE: Australian Ross Baker began collecting clubs as a teenager and is now the go-to expert club maker of replicas. "I was fascinated with the many types, shapes, and concepts people came up with. I haunted Sunday markets, secondhand shops, and antique shops looking for old and interesting golf clubs," he says. His putters are on display at the Australian Golf Club in Sydney and at the Royal Sydney Golf Club. Former Australian governor general Major General Michael Jeffery and Australian golfing legend and 1960 Centenary British Open champion Kel Nagle have both received Baker putters.

square billet of shaft timber by hand until it is round and tapered and in the correct dimension.

A piece of ram's horn is fitted and glued into the leading edge of the putter to protect it. Molten lead is poured into a cavity cut in the rear of the club to give the putter the proper weight. Then Ross cuts a strip of leather for the grip from a full piece of sheep hide. "One putter takes me approximately five hours a day for four days to complete," he adds.

Now Professional and Keeper of the Green at Australia's oldest course, the Ratho Farm Golf Links and Bothwell golf club in Tasmania, Ross creates his clubs in a renovated sheep-shearing shed. "I do it out of love for the craft and love of the game of golf. Money comes way down on the list of things that mean something to me."

BOOKS

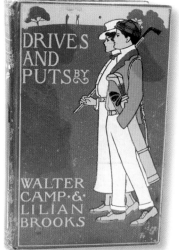

The love of the game will also lead golfing bibliophiles to yearn to start a library. Dealer Tom Stewart advises first establishing a relationship with a reputable seller and counsels would-be collectors never to begin by purchasing books off the Internet.

Entry-level tomes of interest might be *Golf, A Royal and Ancient Game* by Robert Clark, published in 1890; W. W. Tulloch's 1908 book, *The Life of Tom Morris;* and *The Mystery of Golf,* by Arnold Haultain, published in 1908 in a limited first edition.

"Once you begin to collect, you can then specialize into subsets of history, instruction, photography, rules, and architecture," Tom declares, adding that the initial investment in books can range from $200 to $10,000 depending on how much one wants to spend. He strongly recommends the

valuable reference book *The Game of Golf and the Printed Word 1566–1985,* published in 1988, which lists seventy-nine thousand collectible volumes.

It's also important to learn book lingo, like the abbreviations and definitions for the condition of the book and the dust jacket, such as VG/VG and Fine/Good, and the intriguing language of the size of the final printed book: quarto, octavo, duodecimo, sextodecimo, folio, elephant folio, atlas folio, and the giant double elephant folio, which is fifty inches tall.

As collectors add to their golf library, they can trade up for first editions or autographed copies. Notable book dealers specializing in golf are Rhod McEwan in Royal Deeside, Scotland, and Peter Yagi in Redmond, Washington. Bauman Rare Books in New York City and Las Vegas listed a first edition of *Golf Is My Game* inscribed by the legendary Bobby Jones for $6,000.

Lucky seekers may also find a copy of *Following Through* by Herbert Warren Wind, a graceful and respected golf writer who wrote about the game for *The New Yorker.* A signed first edition in fine condition runs about $150, and later reprints can be found for as little as $3.

Also an avid reader, Tom Stewart says the list of great writers past who have been enchanted by golf includes Al Laney of *The Herald Tribune;* P. G. Wodehouse, with a classic collection in *The Golf Omnibus;* John Updike, author of *Golf Dreams;* and George Plimpton, author of *The Bogey Man.*

"Modern writers also have struck golf gold in mining the game in works of fiction and nonfiction," says sports columnist Leonard Shapiro. His recommendations for pure fun to read include books by golf journalist Dan Jenkins, who covered another Fort Worth native, Ben Hogan, as a newspaper reporter, and who wrote the classic *Dead Solid Perfect*, a hilarious piece of fiction focusing on PGA Tour pro Kenny Lee Puckett; the sequel, *The Money-Whipped Steer-Job Three-Jack Give-Up Artist*; and recently, *Jenkins at the Majors: Sixty Years of the World's Best Golf Writing, from Hogan to Tiger.* "Only time will tell how much some of these books will increase in value, but several of Jenkins's first editions now fetch three and four times more than the original prices," adds Shapiro, who recommends the website abebooks.com.

Bestselling author John Feinstein focused on the PGA Tour with *A Good Walk Spoiled*, his first of several golf books. Michael Murphy's *Golf in the Kingdom* introduced the fictional Shivas Irons, a wily Scottish golf professional, to grateful readers; Carl Hiaasen offered another sidesplitting piece of humor with *The Downhill Lie: A Hacker's Return to a Ruinous Sport;* Lorne Rubenstein recounted his golf journey in *A Season in Dornoch: Golf and Life in the Scottish Highlands;* and *Sports Illustrated* writer John Garrity brought his polished prose to the page in *Ancestral Links: A Golf Obsession Spanning Generations.*

OPPOSITE AND ABOVE: Collecting books on golf begins as an innocent first purchase at a book shop or an antique festival and grows into a full-time search. The possibilities for defining one's library include first editions, how-to, and history.

CARING FOR YOUR BOOKS

Once you have amassed a collection of old, new, and rare golf books, keeping them in good shape requires proper care and repair. Controlling the environment is the first step. The two most lethal factors are temperature and bugs. The experts at Brodart Book Supplies in Williamsport, Pennsylvania, warn of mildew: "Also known as mold, it can destroy a book, and it can spread. Indeed, your book is made of organic matter, materials which were alive. The fungi thrive on moisture and heat, so air-conditioning is a good idea." They recommend a special dry cleaning pad against mold.

"Silverfish thrive in dark, warm, moist conditions and are attracted by natural fibers and starchy materials, both of which are plentiful in books," says Don Williams, senior conservator at the Smithsonian Institution. In his book, *Saving Stuff: How to Care for and Preserve Your Collectibles, Heirlooms, and Other Prized Possessions,* he warns, "Cockroaches like to eat something else entirely: They go after the binding glues in the book spine. The two [silverfish and roaches] can make a book or paper collection go away. . . . A closed bookcase is always preferred to help keep critters out."

Guidelines for controlling the environment for books include maintaining a cool and dry atmosphere (do not store books in a damp basement or in a hot, dry attic) and avoiding all sunlight. According to Brodart, nothing can be done to reverse sun damage once books are faded: "The objective is the same as with humans—use a sunscreen; we urge the use of plastic book covers to prevent ultraviolet damage." Williams outlines a three-tiered preservation system according to the age and value of the book. He begins with book covers, moves up to specially fitted acid-free archival storage boxes, and for museum-quality pieces, employs a "Pharaoh's Tomb" using charcoal buffering paper and other materials in an integrated climate control of fifty degrees with humidity at 40 percent.

E IS AN ENTHUIAST, WHO PLAYS EVERY RULE TO THE LETTER, IF HE LEFT BOOKS ALONE HE WOULD PROBABLY PLAY BETTER.

To keep books clean and remove smudges on dust jackets, wipe with a dab of petroleum jelly on a soft, clean cloth. Wipe it off with a cleaning agent like a specialized document cleaning pad. Remedies involving nail polish remover and lighter fluid should be avoided.

In order to remove a label from a book, Brodart recommends Un-Du Label remover, but in a pinch they advise, "Try using a hair dryer. It can be effective in removing price tags or anything that is glued to paper. Set it on low heat. And if your book gets wet, the hair dryer can be a valuable emergency tool for drying. Some also find it effective on beginning mildew."

17

WATER HAZARD

For any golfer traveling to the plumbing capital of Kohler, Wisconsin, to play at the company-owned Whistling Straits, the notion of "draining a putt" definitely takes on new meaning.

Founded in 1873 as a cast-iron foundry by Austrian immigrant John Michael Kohler (1844–1900), the Kohler Company originally specialized in making feed troughs before creating the first enamel bathtub in 1883. When Walter J. Kohler Sr. (1875–1940) took over the company in 1905, he hired the legend-ary Olmsted landscape firm to execute a fifty-year master plan for the village. A second fifty-year master plan was established in 1977 under guidelines from the Frank Lloyd Wright Foundation.

The community of eighteen hundred people maintains a strong focus on ecological concerns,

7 STRAITS COURSE

PAR 3

214

192

176

163

127

HDCP

9

SHIPWRECK

with an emphasis on trees, woodland, and wetland. Now when visitors enter one of the oldest planned communities in the United States and navigate the Olmsted firm's signature circular street patterns, they are treated to an abundance of seasonal horticultural displays. Each autumn the leaves on the trees shimmer in tinges of glowing orange and vibrant red.

Arriving at the vintage American Club main lodge, visitors may stroll beds of bronze, white, and yellow mums, purple kale, lavender, rose hips, and an abundance of gourds and pumpkins in the lodge garden rooms, terraces, and courtyards. Once in their rooms, golfing guests can enjoy the cozy surroundings and a luxurious water experience in each suite, such as the body spa shower, the water tiles shower, and the river bath.

Out on the Pete Dye–designed Irish links challenge called the Straits, duffers will discover an unintentional and much less desirable "water experience." Completed in 1998, the Straits and a second course called the Irish were the brainchilds of Herbert V. Kohler Jr., current chairman of the board and chief executive officer of the company. The 2004 PGA Championship, 2005 Palmer Cup, and 2010 PGA Championship were held at Whistling Straits.

Herbert traveled with Pete Dye to the great courses of Scotland and Ireland before deciding to build a links course by creating dunes on a piece of land that was formerly flat clay. "We spoke quite a bit about the attitude and length," says Herbert. Once Pete set to work, Herbert "didn't mess with him."

Eight holes of the Straits course are hard by the western shore of Lake Michigan, giving golfers ample opportunity to splash a ball into the water at holes such as O'Man, Glory, Cliff Hanger, Pinched Nerve, and the signature seventh, a par three called Shipwreck. A printed guide counsels golfers about this water hazard: "Hitting left is dryer, but not much better." Celtic character also emanates from a flock of forty Blackface sheep that roam the course, providing landscape maintenance and fertilizer.

Golf, water, and a sense of Ireland converge at the rubble-stone-and-slate–covered clubhouse designed by Kohler architect Herb Quast, who incorporated hand-hewn timber supports throughout. "We researched all types of literature on Irish country farmhouses of the 1800s and 1900s, looking at the shape and the materials," Herbert notes. The

PREVIOUS PAGE: The signature hole on the Straits Course in Kohler, Wisconsin, is the aptly named Shipwreck, where any deviation can lead to a ball's landing in a very large water hazard along the western shore of Lake Michigan. OPPOSITE: "The warmth of wood and stone set off by leather and richly patterned fabrics and carpets in traditional patterns are elements that are easily adaptable to a home environment," interior designer Cheryl Rowley says of the men's lounge at Whistling Straits. "There is an easygoing comfort to the design approach."

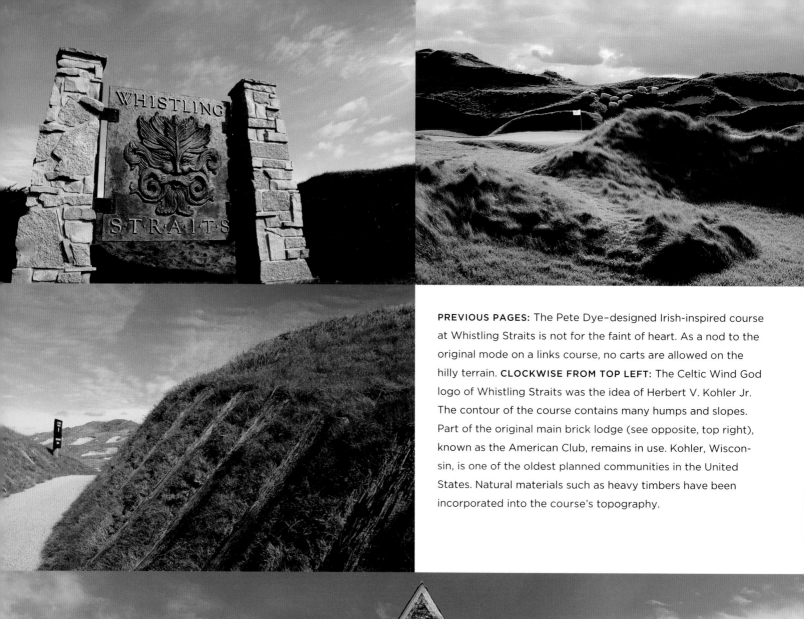

PREVIOUS PAGES: The Pete Dye–designed Irish-inspired course at Whistling Straits is not for the faint of heart. As a nod to the original mode on a links course, no carts are allowed on the hilly terrain. **CLOCKWISE FROM TOP LEFT:** The Celtic Wind God logo of Whistling Straits was the idea of Herbert V. Kohler Jr. The contour of the course contains many humps and slopes. Part of the original main brick lodge (see opposite, top right), known as the American Club, remains in use. Kohler, Wisconsin, is one of the oldest planned communities in the United States. Natural materials such as heavy timbers have been incorporated into the course's topography.

CLOCKWISE FROM TOP RIGHT: The vintage brick American club, which served as the original dormitory for immigrant workers, just across the street from the Kohler factory, is now part of the main guest lodge. The Kohler Company originally specialized in making feed troughs and hog scalders before creating the first enamel bathtub in 1883, ultimately taking bathing way beyond a Saturday-night ritual. "Create an Irish farmhouse" was the design direction expressed by Herb Kohler, president/chairman of the Kohler Company and a passionate golf enthusiast. Thus a team of Kohler architects conceived and created a slate-roofed, timber-framed structure. The Celtic wind logo flaps in his own breeze on a flag at the putting practice area near the clubhouse.

cut stone came from the Halquist Stone quarry just twenty-five miles away.

Beverly Hills–based interior designer Cheryl Rowley added unobtrusive golf style with a fan-shaped arrangement of clubs in the dining room. A lannon stone walkway leads from the dining room to an adjacent champions' locker room used by visiting professionals during major tournaments; here the austere Irish aesthetics are duplicated with enough sinks and showers for the entire field of participants.

The highlight of Whistling Straits is the clubby atmosphere of the men's locker room, with two stone fireplaces, custom Ann Sacks tiles with the "Celtic Wind God" Whistling Straits logo, and lavatory basins featuring artwork that depicts the seventh hole, Shipwreck. Depicting panoramas of the golf course and Lake Michigan, the Kohler Artist Editions sink was inspired by the renowned late-nineteeth-century British artist Douglas Adams and was painted by various artists in the pottery plant. "Why in the world wouldn't we do a golf theme?" Herbert says. "And, there it is."

OPPOSITE: The interiors at Whistling Straits were designed to reflect the same Irish farmhouse tradition. "A rustic, casual elegance infuses the entire project," notes designer Cheryl Rowley. **ABOVE LEFT:** Pale-toned wooden clubs in a fan shape were used as accent points above the cabinets on the wall flanking the mantel. **ABOVE RIGHT:** The Celtic Wind God pops up on everything from the back of a wooden bench to a bottle of house wine.

"We had the luxury of working directly with Kohler to develop custom lavatories for the project," says Cheryl Rowley. For achieving a golf style look at home, she suggests using decorative bowls as tablescapes. "They can be easily adapted to create a unique and individual statement of one's own. Plush, patterned area rugs underfoot would complete the setting.

"Depending upon space and budget limitations, bathroom design can be about the most efficient use of space or the creation of the most luxurious and sybaritic bathing experience," notes Cheryl, who focuses on luxury hotels and resorts. "But if I had to select the most important element to keep in mind when designing a bath, it would be to provide great light, with lots of daylight. A skylight is always a great feature in a bath, as is a garden view."

In the cozy Whistling Straits clubhouse, a crackling fire warms the golfer's soul in late autumn while he relaxes in a leather wingback chair. For those who never want to leave, "the warmth of wood and stone set off by leather and richly patterned fabrics and carpets in traditional patterns are elements that are easily adaptable to a home environment," Cheryl declares.

Following an arduous five-mile trek (since no golf carts are allowed on the course) over rocky, rolling terrain, across windy dunes, over mounds, and through thick tangles of fescue grasses, a hot shower and a return to a much more welcome water experience beckons weary golfers.

OPPOSITE, TOP: The visitors' locker room at Whistling Straits is used by professionals during major events and by members at all other times. OPPOSITE, BOTTOM: Members and guests have a fresh supply of warm towels ready when they return after a rough round on the course. BELOW, TOP TO BOTTOM: The Shipwreck hole has been incorporated into the bathroom sink designs in the men's locker room at Whistling Straits. Designer Ann Sacks created a Celtic Wind God tile for the locker-room showers. Even a blue serpent is part of the water hazard theme in Kohler.

HOW TO AVOID A WATER HAZARD IN YOUR BATHROOM

As a specialist in high-end residential bathrooms and kitchens, Jan Forte of Hume, Virginia, offers tips when considering a new bath or a renovation.

- The man's vanity should be $34^1/2$ inches high plus the countertop; the woman's vanity should be $32^1/2$ inches high plus the countertop.
- In order to avoid a maintenance nightmare, the backsplash for the sink should be the same material as the vanity top.
- The size of the sink should relate to the size of the countertop, and the sink doesn't need to be centered. The sink is best near the front edge to allow clearance at the back for the faucets.
- Using ordinary materials in an unusual way, such as placing square tiles on the diagonal, or ordering stock items instead of custom-made cabinets may help facilitate a conservative budget.
- Become knowledgeable about the mechanics of the room: location of pipes, wires, and even load-bearing walls.
- And finally, the room should be attractive from the other room or rooms; if at all possible, you don't want to see the toilet when the bathroom door is open.

18

It's All About Golf

As the year comes to a close, golfers caught in northern reaches begin to yearn for warmer climes, the better to whack that little dimpled white ball.

Leafing through specialty catalogs and glancing out the window at drifts of snow leads one to conjure a wish list for that jolly old man in the red suit, who might fulfill sweet dreams of a high-tech driver, a can't-miss putter, or a gift certificate for a golf vacation in southern Spain.

Even when Old Man Winter prevents play at certain latitudes, resourceful golfers still find ways to weave their passion into seasonal celebrations. In anticipation of the holidays, Betty Ann Trible blends her newfound fervor for golf with a lifelong love of floral design. The result is a warm and welcoming winter display at her 1890 farmhouse in the Virginia countryside.

PREVIOUS PAGE: Floral designer Betty Ann Trible began with the tan golf bag against the brick surround of the fireplace for her holiday decorations. "I couldn't use it on a table or down the stairs, so I turned to the mantel, which is the largest element and can accommodate the dramatic golf bag feature." ABOVE LEFT: A Plexiglas golf-ball ice bucket is filled with white amaryllis, sprigs of white pine, Trachelium caeruleum (blue throatwort), and a star-of-Bethlehem plant. ABOVE CENTER: Used golf balls were painted silver and tucked into an arrangement with a treasured antique trophy. ABOVE RIGHT: The delicate Virginia boxwood topiary set into a golf-ball basket complements the holiday tablescape. BELOW: During the holidays, it's all about using your imagination to incorporate a golf passion.

"Everybody in my family plays golf, so I decided it was the moment to join them," she says. Carving time out of her busy schedule designing floral arrangements for weddings and special events was the biggest challenge. "I finally came to the point where I found the time now that my children are grown."

With those same children and her grandchildren and friends expected to help celebrate the holidays, Betty Ann decided to decorate in golf style. A red-and-green polka-dot silk ribbon festoons a wreath with sprigs of cedar, juniper, spruce, and cypress at the front door of the house on the circa 1837 Ivanhoe Farm, which once belonged to Fielding Lewis Marshall, a grandson of Chief Justice John Marshall.

A seven-foot fir in the front-to-back center hall sets a festive tone with golf ornaments such as a mini basket of practice balls, a golf bag filled with clubs, and of course a golfing Santa Claus. Gold ribbons encircle the tree, which glitters with twinkling bulbs.

In an adjacent front parlor, Betty Ann uses a vintage khaki canvas golf bag as an anchor for the mantel. The accent pieces are old golf clubs collected by her brother-in-law over many years. "Some were made in St. Andrews, Scotland," she relates. "I knew I wanted to cross the clubs at the top of the mirror as a focal point." A twenty-five-foot-long cypress garland is draped around the edges of a six-foot-tall black-and-gold mirror, purposely uneven. "I don't like things matched and uniform. This is less predictable and adds interest." An extra five feet of the cypress roping is wrapped around the golf bag and puddled on the floor.

From an endless supply of ribbon in her collection, Betty Ann chose a plaid weave. The worn wooden clubs and the shine of the gold edge of the mirror with the plaid present a perfect juxtaposition. "I loved that component of dressed up and dressed

ABOVE: Betty Ann Trible puts the finishing touches on an artichoke arrangement that contains accents of gold-painted golf balls. BELOW: Adorned with golf-ball ornaments and small silver flag pins, a wreath with sprigs of cedar, juniper, spruce, and cypress welcomes guests at Ivanhoe Farm.

down," she says. Winterberry, magnolia, small poinsettias, and large pinecones from a friend embellish the setting.

For a holiday luncheon, Betty Ann sets the table with Mikasa's Christmas Story china and a topiary of Virginia boxwood in a golf ball basket lined with sphagnum moss. Tiny white spray roses and a silver wire ribbon complement the silver golf balls and a miniature antique sterling silver golf trophy at the base of the centerpiece.

Betty Ann also created an artichoke arrangement in a shallow square pine container. "This could be used on a buffet table or as a centerpiece," she explains. Adding glue to the tip, she dipped the artichokes in gold glitter. A votive candle placed in the middle of the artichoke, along with gold golf balls and bits of white pine, bestows an elegant touch on an uncomplicated arrangement.

A polished stainless-steel curio found at a gift shop provides the grand finale for Betty Ann's holiday home makeover. Oasis (a professional floral design foam product that absorbs water and holds flowers in place) serves as a support for sprigs of boxwood that were snipped into a uniform pattern to resemble a shrub. Miniature cordial glasses with golf ball ornaments inside crown the decoration.

Placed discreetly on a small table, it defines the mood: "It's All About Golf."

TOP TO BOTTOM: Found at golf resort gift shops and pro shops around the country, golf-motif ornaments can also double as clever package toppers and hostess gifts.
OPPOSITE: The Southern vernacular of a front-to-back orientation of the center hall provides the perfect setting for Betty Ann Trible's seven-foot fir Christmas tree filled with spheres of silver and gold that echo the form of the silver and gold golf balls incorporated throughout her holiday decor.

THE NINETEENTH HOLE

When it comes to golf, the tradition of libations goes back to David Anderson (1821–1901), a greens keeper and caddy at the Old Course in St. Andrews. Fondly known as Old Daw, he offered weary golfers a ginger beer break at the fourth hole, now known as the "Ginger Beer" hole.

The ritual of congregating in a local pub for a pint of lager after a round of eighteen holes has evolved. Thirsty golfers today sip specialty drinks such as the "Slammer" at the Greenbrier resort in West Virginia; a bartender clad in a red plaid vest (which coordinates with the wall-paper) shakes up two types of bourbon, Bols amaretto, and sloe gin in a chilled beer mug and garnishes the cocktail with an orange slice and a cherry skewered on a golf tee.

Or at Celtic Manor in Cardiff, Wales, a bartender concocts several creative cocktails, such as the "Happy Gilmore" with secret proportions of Kahlúa, Frangelico, and crème de cacao with a sprinkle of cinnamon. Or how about a "Fresh Cut Fairway" with white rum, peach schnapps, apple schnapps, and orange juice?

Cheers!

CLOCKWISE FROM TOP LEFT:
Originally known as a tee box, tee markers now identify the rectangular teeing ground, such as this one with Tom Watson's signature. A bronze image of Sam Snead's trademark hat serves as a yardage marker. A blue elephant emphasizes the Wanderers Club safari theme. Fort Lauderdale Country Club markers are regal, and at Congressional Country Club it's a capitol style. Llamas sometimes carry the golfers' bags at the Talamore Golf Resort, so their image is used as a reminder to golfers near the putting area. The familiar rhododendron at the Greenbrier Resort is not just for imprinting on mugs and china.

RES⊙URCES

www.golfstylebook.com

ON THE ICE, IN THE SHEEP MEADOW, AND TO THE MOON

United States Golf Association
P.O. Box 708
Far Hills, NJ 07931
www.usga.org

Chris Wayne & Associates
Landscapes
15863 97th Drive North
Jupiter, FL 33478-9310
www.chriswayneinc.com

BRUSHSTROKES

Samuel Ingwersen
48 Thurman Avenue
Columbus, OH 43206
www.golfart.org

Henry Koehler
80 North Main Street
Southampton, NY 11968

Surovek Gallery
8 Via Parigi
Palm Beach, FL 33480
www.surovekgallery.com

Charo van Eijck-Aymerich
Chisholm Gallery
P.O. Box 1383
Millbrook, NY 12545
www.chisholmgallery.com

Karen Gehse
21W066 Kensington Road
Lombard, IL 60148
www.karenlovestopaint.com

LeRoy Neiman
Cobalt Artworks
614 West Main Street, Suite 1500
Louisville, KY 40202
www.cobaltartworks.com

Adriano Manocchia
87 Whitecreek Shunpike Road
Cambridge, NY 12816
www.adriano-art.com

Guy Salvato
10278 Olentangy River Road
Powell, OH 43065
www.golfimpressionsplus.com

HOT PANTS AND SPIFFY SPIKES

Ian James Poulter
IJP Design
77-83 Grovebury Road
Leighton Buzzard, Bedfordshire
England
LU7 4TE
United Kingdom
www.ijpdesign.com

Elanbach
Llangoed Hall
Llyswen
Brecon, Powys
Wales
LD3 0YP
United Kingdom
www.elanbach.com

Loudmouth Golf
21911 Hyde Road
Sonoma, CA 95476
www.loudmouthgolf.com

Scottish Tartan Authority
Fraser House, Muthill Road
Crieff, Perthshire
PH7 4HQ
Scotland
United Kingdom
www.tartansauthority.com

E. Vogel Custom Boots and Shoes
19 Howard Street
New York, NY 10013
www.vogelboots.com

THE BUNKER

Carleton Varney
Dorothy Draper & Company Inc.
60 East 56th Street
New York, NY 10022
www.dorothydraper.com

THE FUNK FAMILY OF FLORIDA

Overland Partners
5101 Broadway Avenue
San Antonio, TX 78209
www.overlandpartners.com

Karen Orr Interiors
105 Venetian Boulevard, Suite A
St. Augustine, FL 32095
www.europeanmarketantiques.com

Phantom Screens
30451 Simpson Road
Abbotsford, British Columbia
Canada
V2T 6C7
www.phantomscreens.com

PAPERING THE HOUSE

Thibaut Wallpaper and Fabrics
480 Frelinghuysen Avenue
Newark, NJ 07114
www.thibautdesigns.com

Village Design Group
1495 S U.S. Highway 15-501
Southern Pines, NC 28387-5168
www.villagedesigngroup.com

Mid-State Furniture of Carthage
403 Monroe Street
Carthage, NC 28327

CYMRU A GOLFF

Asbri Golf, Ltd.
Maritime Industrial Estate, Suite 12
Pontypidd
South Wales
CF37 1 NY
United Kingdom
www.asbrigolf.co.uk

Frank Triggs
Triggs Woodforms
The Poplars, Gwern-y-Brenin
Oswestry, Shropshire
Wales
SY10 8AR
United Kingdom
www.woodforms.co.uk

HLN Architects Ltd.
21/22 Neptune Court
Vanguard Way
Cardiff
Wales
CF24 5PJ
United Kingdom
www.hlnarchitects.com

PRETTY IN PINK AND GREEN

Hamilton Tailoring Company
490 E McMillan Street
Cincinnati, OH 45206

World Golf Hall of Fame
One World Golf Place
St. Augustine, FL 32092
www.wgv.com

Lou Lou Button
69 West 38th Street
New York, NY 10018

Replacements, Ltd.
P.O. Box 26029
Greensboro, NC 27420
www.replacements.com

Victoria Park Flowers Studio
901 N.E. 20th Avenue
Fort Lauderdale, FL 33304
www.victoriaparkflowers.com

REES'S MASTERPIECES

Rees Jones
P.O. Box 285
55 South Park Street
Montclair, NJ 07042
www.reesjonesinc.com

Bob Weston
Woodart Studio L.L.C.
300 Grist Mill Drive
Milton, DE 19968
www.rbwoodart.com

Karen Cashman
5920 Horseman's Canyon Drive,
Suite 3A
Walnut Creek, CA 94595
www.karencashman.com

Golf's Golden Years
P.O. Box 842
Palatine, Il 60078
www.golfsgoldenyears.com

BYRDIES

Beverly Olliff
237 Tennessee Avenue
Saint Simons Island, GA 31522

Steven Schoettle
152 Darby Circle
Saint Simons Island, GA 31522

Bevan Funnell
Norton Road
New Haven, East Sussex
England
BN9 0BZ
United Kingdom
www.bevan-funell.co.uk

Josie Kennedy
2110 W. County Line Road
Jackson, NJ 08527

Curry & Co. of Atlanta
294 Deering Road
Atlanta, GA 30309-2290
www.currycodealers.com

F. Schumacher & Co.
79 Madison Avenue, 15th Floor
New York, NY 10016
www.fschumacher.com

ONE MOMENT IN TIME

Pantone
590 Commerce Boulevard
Carlstadt, NJ 07072
www.pantone.com

Tufts Archives
Given Memorial Library
150 Cherokee Road, P.O. Box 159
Pinehurst, NC 28370
www.tuftarchives.org

Zenos Frudakis
200 N. 16th Street
Philadelphia, PA 19102
www.zenosfrudakis.com

SOPHIE'S CHOICES

Frank DuVal
P.O. Box 109
Frederick, MD 21705
www.swingdrawings.com

Cutter & Buck
701 N. 34th Street, Suite 400
Seattle, WA 98103
www.cutterbuck.com

Connoisseur Collection, LLC
9812 Falls Road, 114-#246
Potomac, MD 20854-3963
www.connequestrian.com

Barth and McCallig
469 Seventh Avenue, 12th Floor
New York, NY 10018
www.barthandmccallig.com

Itz a Stitch
8030 St. Martin's Lane
Philadelphia, PA 19118
www.itzastitch.com

Gogie Girl
17100 Halsted Street
Northridge, CA 91325
www.gogiegirl.com

Jeff Keller
138 East 100 North
Logan, UT 84321
www.TheGolfHanger.com

DUFFY'S VINTAGE VANTAGE

Clubhouse Designs
3052 Treadwell Street
Los Angeles, CA 90065
www.clubhousedesign.com

Juliann Schrader
Tee Time Designs
10355 Paradise Boulevard, Suite 811
Treasurer Island, Fl 33706

SWING BLING

Catherine Canino
www.caninojewelry.com

Jewels of Pinehurst
Patricia Reil
7 Market Square
Pinehurst, NC 28370
www.jewelsofpinehurst.com

Mailliard Designs
P.O. Box 1310
Healdsburg, CA 95448
www.mailliarddesigns.com

The Golf Collection
Antique Silver
Marilyn Stevens
661 Date Palm Road
Vero Beach, FL 32963

TREASURERS AND TOMES

Old Sport & Gallery
The Harvard Building
Market Square
Pinehurst, NC 28374
www.oldsportgallery.com

English Accents Antiques
Sally and Wayne Perkins
720 S. Meadow Road
Evansville, IN 47714

Norm Gitzen
8355 Rodeo Drive
Lake Worth, FL 33467
www.normangitzen.com

Marcel Maison
Artmosphere
905 N. Railroad Avenue
West Palm Beach, FL 33401
www.artmosphere.net

Turner Bay Home
4150 North Federal Highway
Fort Lauderdale, FL 33308
www.turnerbay.com

Las Olas Mini Mall
1517 East Las Olas Boulevard
Fort Lauderdale, FL 33301

Bob Pringle
Old Troon Sporting Antiques
49, Ayr Street
Troon
Ayrshire
Scotland
KA10 6EB
United Kingdom
www.golf-art.co.uk

Ross Baker
Ratho Farm Golf Links
P.O. Box 1, Bothwell 7030 Tasmania
Australia
www.rathogolf.com

Rhod McEwan
Ballater
Royal Deeside
AB35 5UB
Scotland
United Kingdom
www.rhodmcewan.com

Peter Yagi Golf Books
16149 Redmond Way, Suite 353
Redmond, WA 98052

Bauman Rare Books
535 Madison Avenue
New York, NY 10022
www.baumanrarebooks.com

Brodart Book Supplies
500 Arch Street
Williamsport, PA 17701
www.brodart.com

WATER HAZARD

The Kohler Company and the
American Club
444 Highland Drive
Kohler, WI 53044
www.kohlerco.com
www.akohlerexperience.com

Cheryl Rowley
446 South Canon Drive
Beverly Hills, CA 90212
www.cherylrowleydesign.com

Ann Sacks
3328 M Street NW
Washington, DC 20007
www.annsackstile.com

Jan Forte
6675 Leeds Manor Road
Marshall, VA 20115

Pratt Larson Ceramics
12200 Northup Way
Bellevue, WA 98005
www.prattandlarson.com

IT'S ALL ABOUT GOLF

Betty Ann Trible
3502 Lea Road
Delaplane, VA 20144
www.designsbybat.com

PH⊙TOGRAPH CREDITS

INDEX